BUILDING RESILIENCE IN CHILDREN AND YOUNG PEOPLE

When children and young people are resilient, they become more confident, curious and adaptable to the world around them. This book provides easy-to-understand, evidence-based strategies to develop children and young people's resilience so they can thrive.

The practical activities and strategies are divided into sections focusing on different aspects of resilience, including emotional awareness, coping with stress, goal setting and problem solving. All activities contain discussion prompts and options for extension and adaptation, and can be used in individual, group and whole-class work. These powerful, cost-effective resources provide an excellent means of developing a structured, whole-setting approach to help children and young people develop the inner toolkit they need to navigate change, manage pressure and recover when things go wrong.

Drawing on research, practice and lived experience, this book is a key resource for teaching staff and educational professionals working with and supporting children and young people.

Nicola S. Morgan is a multi-award-winning TEDx and keynote speaker, international educational consultant, author and teacher. With over two decades of experience in education, she currently works closely with senior leaders, schools and parents and often speaks at conferences on resilience, behaviour management, engaging families, leading through difficult situations and conversations. Nicola taught herself to swim at the age of 37 and a few years later swam the English Channel solo on her second attempt, to prove that anything is possible as long as you believe in yourself.

BUILDING RESILIENCE IN CHILDREN AND YOUNG PEOPLE

A Practical Toolkit to Develop Confidence, Curiosity and Capacity to Cope

Nicola S. Morgan

Routledge
Taylor & Francis Group
LONDON AND NEW YORK

Designed cover image: Getty Images

First published 2027
by Routledge
4 Park Square, Milton Park, Abingdon, Oxon OX14 4RN

and by Routledge
605 Third Avenue, New York, NY 10158

Routledge is an imprint of the Taylor & Francis Group, an informa business

British Library Cataloguing-in-Publication Data
A catalogue record for this book is available from the British Library

ISBN: 978-1-032-52995-0 (hbk)
ISBN: 978-1-032-52994-3 (pbk)
ISBN: 978-1-003-40963-2 (ebk)

DOI: 10.4324/9781003409632

Typeset in Interstate
by Apex CoVantage, LLC

To my mum, Virginia Morgan, thank you for being my unwavering supportive adult over these past few years. You have steadied me through every wobble and gently reminded me to take my warrior's rest when I needed it most. This book simply would not have been written without your constant encouragement over the past few years.

For Charlotte (Charley) Morgan, you are the light in my life and the warmth in my heart. Your energy, smiles and love have carried me through my hardest days. Believe in yourself always Charley. There will be moments that will shake your confidence, but never let them take the fire from your belly. That fire is your motivation, your strength and the quiet proof that you can do anything you set your heart on. For the toughest days ahead, I gift you my mantra: *Head down. Keep going.*

To Isabelle (Izzy) Morgan, you are the light in my life and the comfort in my heart. Your joy, laughter and love have carried me through the toughest days. You are talented in so many ways Izzy, but talent is only the beginning. Everything worth achieving asks for effort, perseverance and hard work. It is what you build through effort that will matter most. You have many gifts, but it is your willingness to try, to keep going and to work for what matters that will shape your future. Remember, nothing worthwhile comes without effort. For those moments when you doubt yourself, I gift you my defining question: *Why not me?*

CONTENTS

ACKNOWLEDGEMENTS

This book has been shaped by the insight, generosity and commitment of many people and I am deeply grateful to all those who have contributed to its development, directly and indirectly.

My sincere thanks go to Dr Lucy Hone for so generously writing the foreword. Lucy's pioneering work in resilience research and applied practice has fundamentally shaped how resilience is understood, taught and lived in both academic and everyday contexts. Her ability to translate robust evidence into humane, accessible and deeply practical insights has been a guiding influence throughout this book. I am grateful not only for her endorsement, but for the clarity, compassion and integrity she consistently brings to the field and for the reminder that resilience is as much about connection and meaning as it is about strength.

My thanks also go to Dr Neil Hawkes, founder of Values-based Education (VbE), whose lifelong commitment to values, character and ethical leadership has profoundly shaped both my thinking and the foundations of this book. Values-based Education sits at the heart of this work, providing the ethical framework through which belonging, behaviour and connection are understood and developed. I am deeply honoured to be an Affiliate of the IVET Foundation and grateful for the trust placed in me to carry this work forward in practical and meaningful ways.

I would like to offer my heartfelt thanks to Professor Ken Reid, OBE who has been both mentor and friend to me for many years. Ken opened the door to academic writing by giving me the opportunity to co-author a number of books and in doing so changed the direction of my professional life. His scholarship, rigour and unwavering expectation of clarity challenged me to think more deeply, write more precisely and hold high standards in translating research into practice. His guidance has shaped not only how I write, but how I think and I am profoundly grateful for his generosity, wisdom and continued encouragement.

I am indebted to Rachel Cooper for her expertise, guidance and constructive challenge throughout my journey to becoming a Resilient Leaders Elements™ (RLE™) Consultant. The Resilient Leaders Elements™ framework is central to this book, providing a clear, evidence-informed structure for understanding and developing resilience under pressure. Her coaching and accreditation strengthened both my personal and professional practice, as well as my confidence in applying these principles with integrity, consistency and purpose.

I would also like to express my deep gratitude to Diana Nyad for her videoed words of encouragement, motivation and belief during preparation for my first English Channel swim attempt. Her reflections on endurance, preparation and psychological resilience, drawn from her own extraordinary experiences, reinforced the central themes of this book, that perseverance is built over time, that setbacks are part of the process and that belief is sustained through disciplined effort rather than momentary motivation. Hearing from someone whose work and lived experience have redefined what is possible offered a powerful source of reassurance and resolve at a critical moment. I am equally grateful to Bonnie Stoll, whose generosity made that connection possible and whose steady, supportive presence reflected the quiet, stabilising strength that sustains us when ambition meets uncertainty. She embodies the kind of grounded encouragement that reminds us we do not achieve difficult things alone.

My sincere thanks also go to Professor Carol Dweck for her encouragement and words of wisdom across both English Channel swim attempts. Her work on mindset has long informed my professional thinking, but her personal generosity, insight and belief during moments of challenge reinforced the very principles this book seeks to explore, that growth is possible, effort matters and setbacks are not endpoints but part of the learning journey.

I would also like to thank Simon Ellis, pilot of *High Hopes* for both English Channel swim attempts, for gifting me the phrase '*unfinished business*'. What began as a moment of insight during those swims has become a powerful and unifying thread throughout this book. It shapes how resilience, perseverance and growth are explored here, not as abstract concepts, but as lived experiences rooted in failure, adaptation and the decision to continue. That single phrase has profoundly influenced how this work reframes setbacks as learning, and endings as beginnings not yet reached.

My sincere thanks go to the practitioners, leaders and families I have worked alongside over many years. Their honesty about what works, what does not and what children and young people truly need underpins every practical element of this book. The examples, reflections and approaches shared here are grounded in those everyday conversations and experiences.

My thanks extend to the schools, colleges, settings and organisations who have welcomed this work into their practice and allowed it to evolve through real-world application. Their willingness to reflect, adapt and prioritise wellbeing alongside learning has been instrumental in shaping the content of this book.

I am grateful to the team at Routledge, Speechmark for their professional guidance, editorial expertise and commitment to publishing practitioner-focused work that is both accessible and evidence-informed. Their support has strengthened this book considerably.

Finally, I would like to thank my family and friends for their patience, encouragement and unwavering support throughout the writing of this book and during one of the most traumatic periods of my life. Their presence, care and belief in both me and the importance of this work sustained me when resilience was not theoretical but lived. This book exists in no small part because they walked alongside me when it mattered most.

FOREWORD

Resilience is a word we use often in education and often get wrong. It is not about toughness, stoicism, a lack of negative emotions, or pushing on regardless of cost. Nor is it something children either possess or lack. Resilience is built. It grows through experience, support, and learning how to respond when things do not go to plan. Understanding how to nurture it in our young people has never been more urgent or important.

Across my career in education as a researcher, practitioner, and author, I have worked with thousands of educators and young people in schools and communities around the world. In this book, Nicola S. Morgan articulates something I see all the time in my work: those who cope best are not the ones who avoid difficulty, but those who learn how to understand it and work with it. The capacity to pause, reflect, adjust, and re-engage, particularly when the way forward feels uncertain, sits at the heart of our ability to function in the modern world. This is why resilience belongs at the centre of education. It shapes wellbeing, behaviour, learning, and our ability to stay engaged when things get hard.

What I value so strongly about this book is Nicola's clear-eyed understanding that resilience is not built through isolated lessons or one-off interventions. Yes, resilience can be taught explicitly, but it also needs to be 'caught' in the everyday interactions and experiences that shape school life (Hone, 2020). It is formed in how adults respond when things go wrong, how predictable and fair systems feel, how safe relationships are, and whether children experience themselves as capable and valued. A whole-school, whole-system approach recognises that every adult, every interaction, and every environment contributes.

Nicola brings both lived experience and strong theoretical grounding to her work. Her account of attempting, and later returning to, the English Channel offers a compelling illustration of how resilience develops in real life. Progress is rarely neat or linear. Pausing is not the same as quitting. Learning how to return matters just as much as learning how to persist. These insights resonate because they reflect how people actually grow through challenge, and Nicola translates them into practical strategies that children and the adults around them can use every day, with immediate effect.

In my own work with schools and communities, I have seen these same skills come to people's rescue time and again, whether in the aftermath of natural disaster, acts of violence, profound personal loss, or the sustained strain of the global pandemic. In those moments, resilience is not theoretical. What makes the difference is whether people recognise what is happening inside them, have practical strategies they can turn to, and know how to use those tools in ways that fit their personality, role, and context. The tools work, but only when people are aware of them, practise them, and learn how to adapt them to their own lives. This is where resilience becomes usable rather than aspirational. If we practise when it is easier, we are better equipped when things are hard.

One of the book's strengths is its attention to what I think of as 'real-time resilience' – the way we choose to think, act, and be in the micro-moments of each day. A child choosing to try again after a setback. A young person deciding to speak rather than withdraw. A pause to steady emotions before reacting. These moments are easy to miss, yet they are where our capacity to cope is quietly built and strengthened through practice. Over time, the rewards of the efforts housed within these choices bolster confidence, emotional regulation, and a sense of agency, all essential for navigating a world that feels increasingly complex and uncertain. Nicola's work helps adults notice these moments and respond in ways that amplify them, rather than letting them slip past unnoticed.

I also appreciate the way Nicola's work is grounded in a clear and compassionate understanding that our capacity to cope resides both *within us* and *between us*. Too often, resilience is presented as an individual trait, something people are expected to summon regardless of their circumstances. Nicola's work resists this oversimplification. Drawing on the work of scholars such as Michael Ungar and Ann Masten, she recognises that resilience is shaped by relationships, environments, and access to support, not just mindset or personal effort. No amount of resilience training will help someone thrive if they are living in their car, repeatedly marginalised, or denied basic safety and dignity. I'm delighted to see this book hold that complexity well.

There is strong alignment here with my own work on whole-school wellbeing. When resilience is embedded into leadership decisions, staff development, curriculum design, and everyday relationships, it becomes part of a school's identity rather than a programme to be delivered. This is where meaningful and sustainable change occurs for children and for the adults who support them. I also appreciated how Nicola's decades of educational experience make her acutely aware of the realities of educational settings. She recognises the pressures educators face, including limited time, competing demands, adult stress, and fragmented approaches. Rather than offering idealised solutions, it provides realistic, evidence-informed guidance that can be woven into existing practice.

Resilience is best understood as both a process and an outcome. It is the way people respond to challenge over time, and the capacity they build as a result. Both matter. In today's pressured environments, we need to support children not only to get through difficulty, but to develop the skills, confidence, and flexibility that allow them to keep learning, adapting, and engaging with life – whatever it throws at them.

This book does exactly that. It is thoughtful, practical, and grounded in both research and experience. It offers educators a credible and compassionate guide for helping children understand that struggle is not a judgement on their ability, but a normal and navigable part of learning and life, and that how we respond, day by day, truly matters.

Dr Lucy Hone

Author of *The Educators' Guide to Whole-School Wellbeing, Resilient Grieving* and *How Will I Ever Get Through This?*

Introduction

Understanding the Importance of Resilience

Resilience is a word we use often, yet our understanding of it continues to evolve. In classrooms, homes and communities across the country children encounter pressures that can unsettle their confidence and stretch their ability to keep going. Long before they have the language to articulate disappointment, change or conflict they are already trying to make sense of what these moments mean for them.

Over the past 28 years, I have worked as a teacher, international education consultant, author and keynote speaker. During that time, I have worked with thousands of professionals, parents and children across a wide range of education settings. No matter the setting, one theme emerges consistently: those who cope most effectively are not the ones who avoid difficulty but the ones who understand it. They are able to pause, reflect and adjust, even when the way forward is unclear.

My understanding of resilience has never come from theory alone; it has been shaped by lived experience, the kind of experience that happens far from any training room. I have failed publicly, painfully and at times spectacularly and I have learned how to draw breath, gather myself and begin again.

In 2017 I attempted to swim the English Channel solo, a 21-mile stretch of unpredictable water that challenges even the most accomplished swimmers. After hours in the cold, I was pulled from the sea before reaching the French coast. Freezing, exhausted and convinced I simply wasn't enough and I believed resilience meant pushing on at any cost.

As our boat turned back towards Dover, the pilot leaned over and said quietly, "We don't call this failure. We call this unfinished business." Those words stopped me. They reframed the experience not as an ending, but as a pause. What I began to understand was that resilience is not always about forcing yourself forward, sometimes it asks you to stop, reassess and repair.

Two years later, after more training, more setbacks and more opportunities to reflect, I returned to the English Channel. After 15 hours, 46 minutes and 47 seconds, I finally reached France. That moment did not simply make me an English Channel swimmer; it changed how I understood resilience. It taught me that progress is rarely linear, that stopping is not the same as quitting and that learning how to return matters as much as learning how to persist.

DOI: 10.4324/9781003409632-1

Since then I have continued to study, teach and speak nationally and internationally on resilience in education settings, organisations and everyday life. As a certified Resilient Leaders Elements™ (RLE™) consultant, I support others to build the clarity, confidence and adaptability needed to strengthen themselves and those around them.

Throughout this journey, there has been one question which has become a constant companion, "Why not me?" and from that "Why not write the book?", "Why not step onto the stage?", "Why not try again when something hasn't worked the first time?" It is a question that interrupts self-doubt, challenges assumption and makes room for possibility. It is also a question we can place into the hands of every child we work with. "Why not them?" "Why shouldn't they lead, create, explore and thrive?" "Why shouldn't they aim high, fall down, stand up and try again?" They can, if we give them the understanding, tools and belief to do so.

My Story, My Why

Growing up as part of a minority community in the 1980s meant learning early that honesty often carried a cost. Difference was something to keep quiet, to manage carefully, to tuck away in order to move through the world unnoticed. What settled in, without me fully realising at the time, was a quiet sense of loneliness. There were moments when shame crept in, not because I believed something was wrong with me, but because the world around me signalled that difference was something to shrink from rather than share.

Exclusion, self-doubt and imposter syndrome were not occasional visitors, they were familiar companions. And yet, each setback offered a lesson. Each disappointment nudged me forward, sometimes walking, sometimes crawling but always learning. Eventually I paused and asked myself a different question, "Why not me?" I realised I had spent years holding myself back with beliefs that were never truly mine. If other people could push past fear and create change, perhaps I could too.

That shift shaped how I see resilience now. Not as an absence of struggle, but as the ability to stay engaged with life even when it feels uncomfortable, uncertain or hard. It is about learning to keep showing up, with curiosity rather than fear and with the understanding that growth often happens alongside difficulty rather than beyond it.

About This Book

This book brings together decades of research, professional practice and lived experience. It is written for teachers, support staff, parents, youth workers and professionals who believe, as I do, that resilience is not something children either have or do not have. It is something we can teach, model and grow with them, day by day and moment by moment.

Life will always involve challenge. It moves in seasons, some lighter, some heavier and nothing stays still for long. Our role is not to shield children from every difficulty, but to help them build the inner toolkit they need to navigate change, manage pressure and recover when things go wrong. Evidence shows that well-designed, education-based programmes can strengthen resilience, emotional regulation and coping skills in meaningful and lasting ways.

This book is about skilling children up for life. It focuses on emotional literacy, self-awareness and practical strategies they can draw on when things feel tough. It helps them understand that challenges are not judgements on their ability, but opportunities for learning and growth.

In my work with schools, colleges and wider education settings, I have seen time and again that behaviour, wellbeing and learning are shaped by one central factor: how we respond when things go wrong. A child who can calm their emotions, regulate their reactions and view mistakes as information rather than identity is a child equipped for life.

Resilience is never one skill, it is a collection of habits, attitudes and choices that strengthen through practice, reflection and supportive relationships. When children learn how to pause before responding, how to meet the challenge within the challenge and how to see failure as unfinished business, they begin to develop a confidence that lasts far beyond the lesson itself.

A Final Word

Life is hard. It is messy, unpredictable and at times deeply unfair. Yet it is also generous, offering moments of joy, hope and connection that remind us why we keep going. Both truths can exist side by side. What remains, over time, are the skills we practise, the strength we discover and the stories we carry forward.

Resilience is not about being unbreakable, it is about understanding that we can rebuild. When children learn to pause, breathe and ask, "What can I learn from this?" they move towards curiosity rather than fear, courage rather than avoidance. They learn that falling is not failure, it is part of becoming.

The units that follow build on the principles introduced here by translating them into practical strategies children can use in real time. Unit 1 begins this process by returning to the English Channel swim story, not simply as a personal narrative but as a structured learning tool. By examining this experience through the lens of resilience research, it shows how moments of uncertainty, disappointment and renewed effort can be used to model coping strategies within education settings. In this way the story becomes a pedagogical resource, bridging lived experience and evidence-informed practice. Units 2 and 3 develop this further by exploring resilience in the education context in more depth and outlining how it can be implemented through a whole-setting approach. Rather than including the structured activities found in the other units, these sections focus on good practice, guidance and practical suggestions for embedding resilience consistently across and throughout the setting.

Throughout this book, the term education setting refers to schools, colleges, youth clubs, alternative provisions and home education. The term 'child' is used collectively to describe children aged 5 to 18. 'Parent' encompasses parents, carers and key family members, while 'adult' refers to teachers, teaching assistants, youth workers, support staff and all those who walk alongside children in their daily lives. The terms SEND (Special Educational Needs and Disabilities) and ALN (Additional Learning Needs) are used throughout to reflect commonly recognised terminology across education systems. All YouTube links and references to frameworks and supporting resources are provided in the Resources section.

Keep in Touch

This work does not end with the final page; it lives on in the conversations you have, the practices you model and the moments when a child surprises you with a spark of confidence you hadn't seen before. I would love to hear how you are using the strategies, frameworks, activities and stories in this book to strengthen resilience and self-belief in the children you work with.

Share your reflections, your challenges, the small wins that felt big. Every experience, yours, mine and theirs adds to the wider ripple of change we are building together. The more we learn from one another, the stronger our collective impact becomes.

Instagram: @nsmtc
Facebook: https://www.facebook.com/NicolaSusanMorgan
Linkedin: https://www.linkedin.com/in/nicola-s-morgan/
Visit: www.nicolasmorgan.com

Unit 1
Understanding Resilience

What this unit covers:

- Understand resilience and reframe setbacks as Unfinished Business to support persistence and confidence.
- Practice key skills such as supportive self-talk, small step planning, emotional regulation and problem solving.
- Complete story-based discussions and activities, including Wobbler versus Warrior reflection and creating a personal Resilience Kit Bag.

Introduction

Helping children and young people develop resilience means preparing them for the reality that learning and progress very rarely follow a straight line. Growing stronger emotionally, socially or academically often happens in the moments when something feels difficult, unfamiliar or doesn't go quite how they hoped. This view is well supported in resilience research, which highlights that growth frequently emerges from experiences of manageable challenge rather than from ease or certainty (Masten, 2014). At the heart of unfinished business is the understanding that a setback is not the end of the story, but a natural and necessary part of the learning journey.

This idea is illustrated through one defining chapter in my life, my solo attempts to swim the English Channel. What began as a physical adventure soon became a deep exploration of how people cope with pressure, uncertainty and the temptation to give up. Research shows that in moments of stress or strain, individuals draw heavily on psychological safety, social support and internal coping strategies to stay regulated and focused (Skinner and Zimmer-Gembeck, 2016). Every hour I spent in the water taught me something about mindset, emotional safety, connection and the confidence that comes from knowing others are cheering you on.

Across both Channel attempts, I experienced first-hand how vital it is to feel psychologically safe when facing a challenge, a finding mirrored in educational research showing that

DOI: 10.4324/9781003409632-2

children are more likely to persist when they feel accepted, supported and understood (Deci and Ryan, 2000). I discovered how supportive relationships protect motivation, how realistic optimism helps individuals stay steady and how problem-solving skills rebuild confidence when challenges feel too big. Studies exploring resilience emphasise that routines, healthy habits and emotional regulation are essential for maintaining balance under pressure (Compas et al., 2017). I also learned how meaning and purpose provides a sense of why something matters and can sustain effort long after comfort disappears, echoing findings from motivation and goal-setting research (Yeager and Dweck, 2012).

My swims mirror what children are asked to do every single day. They must manage pressure, make good choices, stay connected to others, regulate powerful emotions and keep moving forward through difficulties. Studies consistently show that resilience grows through repeated opportunities to practise these skills within safe, supportive environments (Luthar et al., 2015). My experience demonstrates that resilience is strengthened through preparation, community and the courage to adapt. When we help children shift from "I failed" to "I'm not finished yet", they begin to understand that progress can pause without being lost. They learn that reflection, support and a willingness to return to the challenge are fundamental parts of growing stronger.

A key lesson from my Channel experience was the importance of having a planned approach. This training relied on careful assessment of strengths, gaps and emerging needs, followed by targeted adjustments over time. A principle which transfers directly to my work on resilience with children. Just as education settings depend on assessment to understand starting points and structure meaningful learning, resilience development requires us to notice what a child can already do, where they struggle and which strategies will offer the greatest support. Without this planned cycle of assessment, intention and reflection, resilience grows by accident rather than design.

This unit uses the strategies I relied on during my English Channel journey and translates them into everyday tools that children can use. Each idea encourages them to recognise their strengths, manage pressure safely, break challenges into smaller steps and see setbacks as part of learning. The aim is not to recreate the scale of the Channel swim, but to draw on its lessons to support them as they navigate their own moments of unfinished business. The learning I gathered stroke by stroke now forms the foundation for the strategies and approaches included throughout this book.

Discussions to Develop Resilience

The following discussion activities last between 20 and 40 minutes and are designed for children aged 7 to 14, with adaptations made as needed for younger or older children. Each activity is structured under the following headings: Purpose, Instructions, Discussion Prompts, and Extension or Adaptation. It is important to maintain emotional safety by ensuring that all contributions are respected and valued and by reinforcing that resilience grows through experience and reflection rather than through perfection.

Activity: Unfinished Business - Delaying the Urge to Give Up!

Purpose

This activity helps children understand how to manage difficult feelings and delay the urge to give up. By exploring Nicola's real-life English Channel swim, they see that resilience is built through small steps, supportive self-talk and learning from setbacks. The story shows that fear and frustration are normal and that choosing helpful strategies rather than giving up can make challenges feel more manageable.

Instructions

Read Nicola's story aloud or show the TEDx Talk Unfinished Business: Delaying the Urge to Give Up and/or Nicola S. Morgan's Solo Channel Swim 16–17 July 2019 to the group. Ask the children to listen or watch for moments when Nicola felt like giving up and what helped her keep going. Afterwards, lead a short discussion using the questions below. Encourage them to share reflections and connect Nicola's experience to their own challenges.

Nicola's Story

Nicola wasn't a confident swimmer when she was younger. In fact, she didn't learn front crawl until she was 37. She was scared of deep water, hated being cold and even found it hard to swim a few lengths of her local swimming pool.

But in 2016, when she was 43, something surprising happened. A colleague encouraged her to swim the English Channel as part of a two-person relay. Nicola didn't say yes because she thought she was an amazing swimmer, she said yes because she was curious to see what might happen.

Two months later her colleague backed out because the challenge felt too big. Nicola now had a choice, stop or carry on alone. Instead of letting fear decide for her, she chose curiosity, asking "I wonder . . .". She set herself a huge new goal to swim the English Channel solo. This was the moment she began learning deeply about resilience, mindset and never giving up.

The First Attempt

In August 2017, Nicola tried her first solo swim across the English Channel. She swam for 14½ hours, until a strong current grabbed her and held her in the same spot for two whole hours. She didn't move an inch; for her safety the boat pilot decided to pull her out of the water. Wrapped in a sleeping bag, Nicola felt heartbroken; she didn't feel brave, she felt like she had failed. Then the pilot said something that changed everything. He said, "We don't call this failure. We call this unfinished business." His words helped her calm down and think clearly; instead of giving up, she went home determined to try again. She reviewed her training, asked experts for advice, reconnected with her support team and began visualising a second attempt.

The Second Attempt

Two years later, in July 2019, Nicola stood on Dover beach again. This time she was stronger and more prepared. She had trained in cold lakes and the sea, lifted weights, taken ice baths and rested properly. But two hours into the swim, in complete darkness, that worrying voice in her head said "You're not good enough. Only amazing swimmers do this. Just stop and get on the boat." Nicola didn't pretend the voice wasn't there. Instead, she used a strategy she had practised and she said to that voice: "You can get out if you want to Nic . . . but not now. You can get out when the sun comes up."

This made the challenge feel smaller. She didn't promise to swim the whole Channel. She just promised to swim until sunrise. When the sun finally rose and warmed her back, she thought, "I can do this." She looked towards France and imagined her feet touching the beach.

Challenges Inside the Challenge

Daylight didn't magically make everything easy. Nicola swam into jellyfish and, when she pushed one away, she damaged her shoulder. The pain shot through her arm, but she remembered her tools - use self-awareness, solve the problem in front of you and take small steps - so she said to herself "Just swim for 30 minutes, then you can have some liquid food."

Thirty minutes felt manageable; that small promise kept her calm and moving forward. She also changed her focus: instead of thinking only about the pain, she looked closely at the jellyfish. They were bright and colourful, all different shapes and sizes. When she focused on their beauty, she felt lucky to be swimming among them, even though it still hurt, especially when one wrapped around her wrist.

She learned that perseverance doesn't mean pretending everything is fine. It means staying safe, using your strengths and choosing what to pay attention to. Her support crew cheered from the boat, reminding her that having people who believe in you really matters.

Unfinished Business Completed

Just over halfway across, Nicola was exhausted. Her shoulder throbbed. She felt cold and had been sick from swallowing seawater. Lifting her arm was getting harder, but every time she stopped for food, her friend on the boat said "You've got this, Nic. You knew it would be hard. If it were easy, everyone would do it. Now head down, keep going." So that's what she did, "head down, keep going".

Huge ships passed by, her crew cheered, held up messages on a whiteboard and gave her treats like chocolate mousse, warm drinks and jelly babies all passed to her in a fishing net or tied to a long bit of string so she didn't touch the boat. Nicola kept herself going with mental exercises, she did a body scan, counted her breaths, imagined telling people she was an English Channel swimmer.

After 14 hours, her crew shouted that they could see France. "Head down, keep going Nic!" Fishing boats bobbed nearby, jellyfish drifted next to her and a seal even popped up to say hello. When she was one mile from the beach, two people from her crew jumped into the water in their wetsuits to swim behind her. Their support helped her push through the final stretch. As she got closer, she could see the sandy seabed rising up, until she finally reached a place where she could stand; she stumbled a few times but kept going. People on the beach stood up and cheered as Nicola walked out of the water.

When her feet touched dry sand, the boat pilot sounded the hooter, the official signal. Nicola had done it. She was now an English Channel swimmer. She completed the crossing in 15 hours, 46 minutes and 47 seconds.

English Channel Swim Facts

People often call swimming across the English Channel the Mount Everest of swimming, because it is one of the hardest swims in the whole world. The Channel is the stretch of sea between England and France.

Even though the shortest distance is about 21 miles (34 kilometres), swimmers can't just swim straight across. The sea has very strong tides and currents that push them sideways, so most people end up swimming much further, sometimes as far as 35 miles.

The water is also extremely cold; even in summer it is usually only around 14°C to 18°C. Because of all these challenges, only about 1 in 3 swimmers manage to make it all the way across. It is said that more people have climbed Mount Everest than have completed this swim. The English Channel is one of the busiest shipping areas in the world, with more than 500 big ships passing through the Dover Strait every single day.

Famous English Channel Swimmers

Captain Matthew Webb was the first person ever to swim across the English Channel. He did it in August 1875, and it took him 21 hours and 45 minutes of nonstop swimming.

Gertrude Ederle was the first woman to swim across the Channel. She completed her swim on 6 August 1926, going from France to England in 14 hours and 34 minutes. She didn't just break a record, she beat the men's fastest time by almost two hours. Her story was adapted for the film *Young Woman and the Sea, 2024.*

Record-Breaking Swimmers

Sophie Etheridge took the longest time to complete a successful one-way swim, taking 29 hours and 4 minutes, in August 2023, which was more than an entire day of swimming. Andreas Waschburger holds the record for the fastest one-way solo swim. On 8 September 2023, he swam from Dover to France in just 6 hours, 45 minutes and 25 seconds.

Discussion Prompts

To help the group explore the challenges in Nicola's story and connect them to their own experiences, use the following discussion questions and prompts.

Understanding the Challenge

- What words would you use to describe how hard it is to swim across the English Channel?
  Prompt: Think about how the water might feel, how long the swim is and what it would be like to keep going for hours. What words come to mind?
- Why do you think people say swimming the English Channel is like climbing Mount Everest?
  Prompt: Both are huge challenges that only very determined people try. Why might people compare a long, cold swim to climbing the tallest mountain in the world?
- How do you think the swimmer might feel, knowing that most people who try don't make it all the way across?
  Prompt: Imagine you were about to try something really difficult that many people couldn't finish. What feelings might you have?

Connecting to Personal Experience

- Can you think of a time when something in your life felt like your own "Mount Everest", something that felt really big or really hard at first?
  Prompt: Maybe it was learning a new skill, joining a new group, doing a hard piece of schoolwork or trying something for the first time.
- What helped you to keep going when things got difficult?
  Prompt: Did someone support you? Did you practise more? Did you talk to someone or try a new way of doing it?
- How did you feel when you finally made progress or reached your goal?
  Prompt: Think about the moment when things started to get easier or when you did something you didn't think you could do. What emotions did you have?

Exploring Qualities of Resilience

- What physical and mental qualities do you think someone needs to swim the English Channel?
- Prompt: Think about the swimmer's body and their mind. What might they need?
- Which of those qualities do you already have? Which ones would you like to get better at?
- Prompt: Everyone has some strengths already. Which ones feel like yours? And which ones would you like to grow or practise more?
- What could help you build those qualities in everyday life?
- Prompt: What small things could you do at your education setting, at home or with friends to become stronger, calmer, braver or more determined?

Learning from Setbacks

- Only one in five swimmers reaches France. What does this tell us about resilience and persistence?
  Prompt: Why do you think people keep trying even when it's really hard? What does this show about not giving up and staying strong, even when the chances of success are small?

- If a swimmer has to stop before finishing, does that mean they have failed?
  Prompt: Think about all the training, courage and effort they put in. Does stopping early take away everything they achieved along the way?
- How might the idea of "unfinished business" help someone who wants to try again after a setback?
  Prompt: Imagine thinking, "I didn't finish yet, but I can come back stronger next time." How could this way of thinking help someone keep going and have another try?
- What obstacles or "rough waves" might you face on the way?
  Prompt: These could be challenges like tricky schoolwork, worries, mistakes, busy schedules, or moments when you feel like giving up.
- Who could be part of your support team to help you keep going?
  Prompt: Think about the people who encourage you or help you when things get hard, family, friends, teachers, coaches or trusted adults.
- How can you remind yourself to "keep swimming" when life's waves get strong?
  Prompt: What could you do or say to yourself to stay motivated?

Extension or Adaptation Options

For younger children, use simple drawings or symbols to show the challenge and the small steps that help them keep going. Practise short coping phrases such as Not yet or One more try to delay the urge to give up. For older children, ask them to write about a time they wanted to quit and reframe it as Unfinished Business by identifying what they learned and what they will try next time. In group settings, create a Keep Swimming wall where children add helpful self-talk, small step ideas and support team reminders. Invite a trusted adult to complete a short support plan with the child, focusing on what helps them stay motivated when things feel hard.

Activity: The Power of Three

Purpose

The purpose of this session is to introduce children to key resilience concepts, unfinished business, Wobblers and Warriors and the challenge within the challenge, which together form the resilience kit bag. These ideas help them understand how to keep going when things feel difficult, how to manage setbacks safely and how to return to challenges with confidence.

Instructions

Before beginning any of the discussions in this session, ensure that children watch the TEDx Talk Unfinished Business: Delaying the Urge to Give Up by Nicola S. Morgan (2023) in full. This provides a shared starting point and helps them understand the key messages, stories and examples that the session builds upon.

Discussion Prompts: Unfinished Business

Use these prompts to help them explore what unfinished business means and how it can encourage them to keep going when things get tough.

- What do you think unfinished business means in your own words?
- When something goes wrong, how could thinking about it as unfinished business help you keep trying?
- Can you remember a time when you kept going and finished something, even though it felt really hard?
- Do you think being resilient always means keeping going no matter what, or can it sometimes mean stopping to stay safe and try again later?
- Can you think of a time when taking a break or stopping helped you come back stronger or make a better decision?

Discussion Prompts: Wobbler and Warrior

Use these discussion prompts to help them talk about their own Wobbler moments, Warrior moments and the ways they rest and recover after a challenge:

- Can you remember a time when something felt so hard that you wanted to stop?
- What was your Wobbler voice saying to you then?
- What helped you to keep going even a little bit?
- Do you think someone can wobble and be a warrior at the same time? Why do you think that?
- What do you like to do for your Warrior's Rest to help yourself calm down, recover or feel better after something challenging?

Discussion Prompts: Challenge within the Challenge

Use these questions to help them talk about the surprise challenges they face and how they cope with them:

- What hidden challenges have you faced lately?
- How did they make you feel?
- What could help you stay steady next time?
- Can you remember a time when a tricky bit inside a bigger challenge helped you learn something about yourself?
- When something unexpected happens, what's the first thing you do, and how does it help you?

Extension or Adaptation Options

For younger children use simple picture prompts to explain unfinished business, Wobblers and Warriors and the challenge within the challenge, for example a wobble cloud and a warrior shield. Keep questions short and offer choices such as "Was that a Wobbler moment or a Warrior moment?" For older children, ask them to write or talk about a real situation and identify their Wobbler voice, their Warrior response and what Unfinished Business would look like next time. In group settings, create a Resilience Kit Bag wall where children add examples of helpful self-talk, support strategies and ways to rest and recover after challenges. Invite children to role play a Wobbler to Warrior moment and practise switching from unhelpful thoughts to a steadier, more confident response. Encourage a trusted adult to support this at home by helping the child name their Wobblers, choose a Warrior phrase and plan a simple rest and reset routine.

Activity: My Resilience Kit Bag

Purpose

The purpose of this activity is to help children recognise that resilience can be learned, strengthened and personalised. By creating their own Resilience Kit Bag, they begin to identify the strategies, techniques and tools that support them when things feel difficult. This activity encourages them to build a growing collection of ideas they can return to whenever they face challenges.

Instructions

Explain to children that everyone can create their own Resilience Kit Bag, a place to store strategies that help them keep going, stay steady and move forward from setbacks. Invite them to choose ideas that feel realistic and useful for them. They can write or draw the contents of their kit bag on a sheet of paper, or they can design and make a physical kit bag using craft materials.

Let them know that this kit bag will continue to grow each time they complete a new activity in the programme, they will have the chance to reflect on what they found helpful and decide whether they want to add it to their kit bag. Encourage them to make it personal, meaningful and something they can use in everyday life.

Discussion Prompts

Use these discussion prompts to help them explore the importance of having a Resilience Kit Bag.

- What things did Nicola use to help her keep going during her swim?
- Which of those things do you remember the most and what made it stand out for you?

- Do you think any of Nicola's ideas could help you when something feels difficult?
- What helpful things do you already do that you'd like to put in your own Resilience Kit Bag?

Extension or Adaptation Options

For younger children, offer picture choices and simple labels for their kit bag such as calm breathing, helpful words, take a break and ask for help and let them draw the tools instead of writing. For older children, encourage them to create a personalised kit bag with clear examples of when and how they would use each strategy, including a Wobbler thought and a matching Warrior response. In group settings create a shared Resilience Kit Bag display where children contribute ideas and learn new strategies from each other. Invite children to practise choosing one tool from their kit bag for a real-life scenario and explain why it would help. Where appropriate, involve a trusted adult by asking them to add one supportive strategy they notice works well for the child at home, helping to build consistency across settings.

Connecting the Learning

Nicola's experience shows the universal processes that underpin resilient behaviour, staying regulated under pressure, drawing strength from relationships, keeping a clear purpose and choosing helpful thinking when things feel tough (Masten, 2014). These same processes shape how children cope with challenge in their settings, at home and in their communities. Throughout this unit Nicola's English Channel swims have illustrated that resilience is built between setbacks, recovery and renewed effort. Her personal challenge became a study in how preparation, mindset and connection turn overwhelming situations into manageable steps.

The lessons she learned about safety, belonging, optimism, problem solving, healthy habits and emotional regulation form the foundation for the strategies in this book. By sharing her story of unfinished business, Nicola shows that resilience is not about avoiding mistakes, but about pausing, reflecting and beginning again. When children shift from "I failed" to "I am not finished yet", they start to see resilience as something strengthened through practice, support and courage (Yeager and Dweck, 2012).

This is why a Resilience Kit Bag sits at the heart of the programme. Nicola completed her swim by breaking challenges into small steps, calming her body through routines, choosing where to place her attention, drawing strength from her support team and reconnecting with her purpose. Each unit adds similar tools that help children steady themselves when life becomes difficult.

Unit 1 has introduced these ideas through lived experience, giving everyone a shared language and practical starting point. The next unit builds directly on this foundation by shifting the focus from the individual to the environment. Unit 2 explores how relationships, routines, expectations and partnership with families work together to create the conditions in which every child can develop their own unfinished business mindset (Hamre and Pianta, 2006).

In this way, the opening story becomes a bridge into understanding how resilience is strengthened across whole systems, not only within individuals. As the programme moves into Unit 2, the focus turns to the environments that surround children and to how education settings can actively cultivate resilience every day.

Unit 2
The Role of Resilience in Education

What this unit covers:

- Understand resilience as a developing skill and why it matters for children's wellbeing, behaviour and learning.
- Identify key resilience factors and barriers, including emotions, routines, relationships, mindset and problem solving.
- Practise classroom strategies and reflection tasks to build resilience and review impact across the setting.

Introduction

Children today are growing up in a world that often feels faster, louder and more changeable than the one many adults remember. Research shows that rising levels of social pressure, rapid technological change and uncertainty all shape how children feel and behave (Blakemore, 2018). For some this creates opportunities and excitement, but for others it can unsettle their sense of security and make everyday learning tasks feel harder to manage.

Children tend to cope best when surrounded by adults who offer warmth, consistency and clear expectations. This approach reflects the authoritative style described in developmental research, which is associated with improved behaviour, stronger resilience and better learning outcomes (Baumrind, 1991; Pianta, Hamre and Allen, 2012). When adults provide this steady balance, children experience a sense of safety that makes challenge feel manageable rather than overwhelming. When the balance is missing, uncertainty can become a barrier to engagement and wellbeing.

This unit introduces resilience as an ability that develops over time through experience and support. Research describes resilience not as a fixed trait but as a dynamic process shaped by internal strengths and the relationships and environments surrounding a child (Masten, 2014; Ungar, 2012). This understanding aligns with ecological perspectives that emphasise the combined influence of school, home and community on development (Bronfenbrenner, 1979).

DOI: 10.4324/9781003409632-3

In practice, resilience strengthens when children encounter manageable challenges while knowing that trusted adults are present, understanding and available.

Resilience is not about expecting children to cope alone or trying to make them tougher. It involves equipping them with secure relationships, emotional tools and steady encouragement so that difficulty feels possible to manage (Luthar, Crossman and Small, 2015; Hart and Blincow, 2007). The aim of this unit is to offer clear, practical guidance to help adults build these foundations through everyday interactions, routines and consistent relational support.

Understanding Resilience

Resilience is best understood as something children learn and build, rather than a fixed quality they either have or lack. Research reminds us that children become more resilient when they tackle manageable challenges while feeling noticed, supported and steady in the presence of reliable adults (Masten, 2001; Luthar, Cicchetti and Becker, 2000). Over time, these everyday experiences interact with a child's biological, environmental and relational influences, shaping how they respond when life becomes difficult.

In practice, resilience can be seen developing in small, often easily missed moments. A child deciding to try again after a disappointment. A teenager choosing to talk something through rather than shutting down. A younger child pausing to breathe when frustration rises. These brief experiences help children understand that difficulties can be worked with rather than avoided, gradually strengthening confidence, emotional balance and coping skills (Rutter, 2013; Siegel, 2012).

Resilience grows further when children can draw on two things: their own developing inner resources and the supportive structures around them. Inner resources include skills such as problem solving, noticing and managing feelings and holding a realistic sense of hopefulness (Bandura, 1997). External supports, trusted adults, predictable routines and opportunities to feel part of a community provide the sense of safety and belonging children need when facing challenge (Werner and Smith, 2001). A clear sense of purpose also helps many children stay motivated when things feel tough (Benard, 2004).

Together, these elements do not remove adversity, but they help children face it without becoming overwhelmed. For adults the key is to notice and nurture the small steps, the moments when a child risks trying again, asks for help, or tolerates a feeling they would once have avoided. By responding calmly, offering steady guidance and celebrating progress, adults play a crucial role in helping resilience take root.

Why Resilience Matters in Today's World

Children today are growing up in a fast-moving world shaped by technology, shifting social expectations and a constant flow of information. These changes bring opportunities, but many children also describe feeling under more pressure and being more aware of comparison than ever before (Twenge, 2017; Odgers and Jensen, 2020; Blakemore, 2018). Education settings see this reflected in the classroom through higher levels of worry, difficulty managing strong feelings and a growing reluctance to try something new (NHS Digital, 2023; Loades et al., 2020).

When children are still learning how to name their emotions or make sense of challenge, it can be harder for them to stay engaged. Stress naturally affects thinking skills such as working memory, focus and problem solving. This can leave children feeling stuck, confused or easily overwhelmed (Ochsner and Gross, 2005; Gathercole and Alloway, 2008).

Resilience supports children to keep going when something feels difficult. It helps them feel safer emotionally, strengthens relationships by making repair and communication easier and encourages curiosity and adaptability in their learning (Masten, 2014; Ungar, 2012; Yeager and Dweck, 2012; Deci and Ryan, 2000). In a world that continues to change quickly, the ability to cope, adapt and stay open to learning is not just helpful; it is essential for children's wellbeing and progress, both now and in the future (OECD, 2019).

Barriers to Building Resilience

Barriers to resilience can arise even in well intentioned and supportive settings. Recognising them early helps adults respond with confidence and compassion. One common challenge is when the focus shifts too heavily toward performance. When children feel that getting things right matters more than learning itself, they can become hesitant to try new approaches or take risks (Dweck, 2006). In everyday practice, this might show up as a child avoiding a task they worry they will struggle with. Gentle reassurance, clear modelling and valuing effort can help ease this pressure.

Busy curriculum expectations can unintentionally squeeze out time for emotional learning. When time is tight, resilience-building activities may feel optional, even though they underpin children's capacity to cope with setbacks (Weare, 2015). Making space for brief, regular check-ins or reflective conversations can help integrate emotional learning back into daily routines.

Adult modelling is another key factor. When adults feel exhausted or under strain, it becomes harder to demonstrate the calm, steady responses children need to see (Jennings and Greenberg, 2009). Noticing these moments and seeking support, whether through team reflection, supervision or shared problem solving helps adults maintain the consistency that builds trust.

Relationships between home and the setting also influence resilience. Limited communication or missed opportunities to connect can lead to children receiving mixed messages about expectations and support (Epstein, 2011; Sheridan et al., 2019). Simple, regular touchpoints with families can strengthen the sense of continuity children rely on.

Finally, systemic inequalities such as financial hardship, discrimination or unstable living circumstances create ongoing stress for some children. These pressures do not diminish their potential for resilience, but they increase the importance of stable, attuned relationships (Evans and Kim, 2013). When adults understand the wider context, they are better placed to respond with empathy and provide the steady, nurturing environment that helps resilience grow (Masten, 2014). By recognising these barriers, adults can take small, purposeful steps to create conditions in which every child has the chance to develop the resilience they need to thrive.

Practical Strategies for Educators

The following strategies offer realistic, everyday ways for adults to strengthen resilience across education settings. Each strategy includes a clear focus, a practical application and reflective prompts adults can use individually or in teams.

Embedding emotional literacy provides the foundation for resilient behaviour, as children are far better equipped to manage their feelings when they can first recognise and name them (Denham, 2006). Simple, everyday practices such as daily check-ins, using clear visuals or familiar language, brief reflective pauses during transitions and accessible co-regulation strategies like breathing routines or sensory tools help them tune into their emotional state without fear of judgement (Perry, 2006; Siegel, 2012).

These moments create space for calm, enabling adults to guide children back towards regulation before emotions escalate (Porges, 2011). Developing emotional literacy further strengthens self-awareness, supporting smoother learning and relationships by helping them recognise what is happening internally and what might help next. By examining how emotions appear day to day, identifying routines that already support awareness and noticing opportunities for brief check-ins, adults can design approaches that are both thoughtful and compassionate (Jennings and Greenberg, 2009).

MODELLING ADAPTIVE THINKING

Focus: Modelling adaptive thinking is one of the most powerful ways adults can nurture resilience, as children take their cues from how adults handle challenge, frustration and uncertainty (Bandura, 1986). Speaking our thinking aloud, acknowledging when something has not gone as planned and calmly considering the next step, demonstrates that setbacks are manageable rather than threatening (Flavell, 1979).

Practical Application: Using growth-oriented questions such as "What might help next time?" and recognising effort alongside outcomes reinforces the understanding that learning is a process rather than a performance (Dweck, 2006). These everyday interactions shape the internal dialogue children develop about themselves and their abilities.

Reflection: Reflecting on the messages they hear during difficult tasks and on whether the language used signals possibility rather than perfection, supports adults to model the flexible mindset they wish children to develop (Jennings and Greenberg, 2009).

CREATING PREDICTABLE, SUPPORTIVE ENVIRONMENTS

Focus: Predictable, supportive environments provide the emotional steadiness children need to settle, focus and build trust in the adults around them (Perry, 2006). When routines are easy to understand and consistently followed, children spend less energy trying to work out what will happen next and more energy engaging with learning (Eccles and Roeser, 2011; Sugai and Horner, 2006). Clear expectations, presented calmly and confidently, help children feel that adults will respond with fairness rather than frustration (Jennings and Greenberg, 2009).

Practical Application: A helpful principle for maintaining relationships is 'connect before correcting'. Taking a brief moment to acknowledge how a child is feeling before giving guidance shows that their emotions matter, even when boundaries are needed (Pianta, 1999; Siegel and Bryson, 2014). This simple pause often reduces defensiveness and allows them to hear what comes next.

Reflection: Adults can also reflect on the parts of the day that feel least predictable for children. Transitions, busy corridors or unstructured times may heighten worry or prompt reactive behaviour. Considering where small adjustments to routines, visual cues or adult presence could ease pressure helps ensure systems genuinely support children rather than overwhelm them.

Creating this blend of safety and structure is not about rigid control, it is about offering a steady, reassuring rhythm to the day. When children know what to expect and feel understood, their capacity to learn, communicate and manage challenges increases.

STRENGTHENING BELONGING AND CONNECTION

Focus: A strong sense of belonging is central to resilient development. Children gain confidence when they know they are noticed, valued and kept in mind by the adults around them (Baumeister and Leary, 1995; Masten, 2014).

Practical Application: This is built through small, everyday actions. Greeting a child by their name, acknowledging their effort or commenting on something they have done well helps them feel seen. Offering regular opportunities for them to contribute ideas, help shape routines or take on simple leadership roles shows that their voice matters (Hattie and Yates, 2014; Deci and Ryan, 2000).

These consistent messages of acceptance help children understand that they hold an important place in the life of the setting (Scales et al., 2018). A useful starting point is to consider whether each child has at least one trusted adult they can turn to. Reflecting on who may be slipping into the background, or who appears quieter or less connected than usual, allows adults to respond early and thoughtfully (Werner and Smith, 2001). Even a brief check-in, a shared task or a few minutes of one-to-one encouragement can begin to close the gap.

Reflection: When adults intentionally notice, listen and respond, the setting becomes a place where children feel secure enough to manage challenges without feeling alone. These relationships form the foundation on which resilience can grow (Ungar, 2012).

ENCOURAGING PURPOSE AND CONTRIBUTION

Focus: Encouraging purpose and contribution is a powerful way to deepen resilience, as children thrive when they feel that what they do carries weight and meaning (Damon, 2008).

Practical Application: When education settings create opportunities for them to take on roles such as peer mentors, participate in community-based projects or lead their own initiatives that emphasise teamwork and service, they reinforce the message that every child has something valuable to offer (Lerner et al., 2005; Eccles and Gootman, 2002).

Reflection: These experiences help them connect effort with influence, showing how their actions shape outcomes for themselves and others (Bandura, 1997). Reflecting on whether they are given regular, meaningful chances to contribute and how often they are supported to notice the impact of their involvement enables adults to strengthen this sense of purpose (Scales et al., 2018). Children subsequently learn that their voice matters, their actions count and they can make a meaningful difference, even in small but significant ways (Deci and Ryan, 2000; Zeldin, Christens and Powers, 2013).

DEVELOPING COGNITIVE AND PROBLEM-SOLVING SKILLS

Focus: Supporting children to think clearly, plan ahead and make considered choices is a core part of building resilience. When children are taught how to break down a task, reflect on what is happening and choose a sensible next step, they are better equipped to manage challenge with increasing independence. Research into executive functions highlights the value of strengthening skills such as planning, flexibility and reflective thinking, as these processes underpin purposeful decision making (Diamond, 2013; Zelazo and Carlson, 2012).

Practical Application: In everyday practice, this means creating regular opportunities for children to solve manageable problems and talk through their thinking. Simple routines such as setting a small goal for a lesson, reviewing what worked well, or comparing possible solutions help them notice the link between actions and outcomes (Zimmerman, 2002). These approaches also give adults and children a shared language for slowing down, considering options and adjusting plans when things feel uncertain (Flavell, 1979).

Reflection: When adults look closely at the moments children genuinely get to make decisions, however small, they can identify where practice might be refined. Encouraging children to explain what helped them succeed and why, strengthens their ability to think their way through difficulty rather than relying on adult direction (Bransford, Brown and Cocking, 2000). Over time, this consistent focus on noticing, choosing and reviewing helps children develop the steady, confident problem-solving skills that support resilience across learning and life.

INVOLVING FAMILIES AND COMMUNITIES

Focus: When families and education settings work side by side, children experience a powerful sense of consistency that strengthens their ability to cope, learn and thrive (Epstein, 2011; Sheridan et al., 2019). Effective partnership is built through regular, strengths-focused communication that highlights what is going well and invites families into the learning journey.

Practical Application: Practical opportunities such as workshops on emotional coaching or establishing calm learning routines help to align approaches at home and education setting, while wider community partnerships ensure that provision reflects the culture, identity and resources of the local area (Ladson-Billings, 1995).

Reflection: Taking time to reflect on current patterns of engagement and considering the strengths that already exist within the community, allows adults to build on what is trusted and familiar (Mapp and Kuttner, 2013). In doing so, education settings create a network of adults who share responsibility, speak a common language and offer children the stable, joined-up support they need.

EVALUATING AND REFLECTING ON IMPACT

Focus: Evaluating how resilience is developing across a setting works best when it becomes part of everyday practice rather than a separate initiative. Education settings and early years settings are already balancing many priorities, so any approach to evaluation needs to feel manageable and purposeful. The aim is not to create more work but to help adults understand what is changing, where support is still needed and how children are experiencing daily life.

Practical Application: A simple four-stage cycle can guide this process. The first question, "Where are we now?", invites adults to look honestly at current wellbeing information, observations from the classroom and the voices of children and families. This provides a grounded starting point. The second question, "Where do we want to be?", encourages them to build a shared, practical picture of what resilient behaviours look and sound like for children in your setting. Many settings find it helpful to describe these behaviours in everyday terms, such as noticing when a child keeps trying with a tricky task or seeks help appropriately.

The third stage, "How will we get there?", focuses on identifying a small number of realistic priorities. These may include strengthening adults' confidence in modelling calm responses, weaving resilience skills into the curriculum or building positive relationships with parents. Keeping the focus tight helps adults feel supported rather than overwhelmed. Finally, "How will we know it is working?" brings attention to the evidence that matters most. This might be attendance and engagement data, but equally valuable are the stories, comments and moments that show how children and families feel within the setting.

Reflection: Reflection should give adults space to learn with and from one another. When adults feel confident, connected and encouraged, they naturally model the collective resilience that children rely on every day.

Connecting the Learning

Resilience is not a fixed trait; it develops through relationships, routines and the everyday interactions that help children feel safe and supported (Luthar, Cicchetti and Becker, 2000). Children build resilience when adults provide calm, consistent responses and create an environment where it is acceptable to try, make mistakes and try again (Masten, 2014; Werner and Smith, 2001). When education settings, families and communities work together with shared expectations and a clear sense of belonging, children gain the confidence to cope with challenges and to continue learning (Scales et al., 2018). Over time, these regular experiences help children recognise their own strengths and understand that they are not facing difficulties alone.

This unit has shown that resilience grows through predictable routines, supportive relationships and opportunities for children to contribute. For adults, this means offering steady emotional responses during difficult moments, modelling curiosity rather than judgement, giving children regular opportunities to practise coping skills in manageable steps and maintaining consistent expectations across all adults involved in their care.

When adults use these approaches together, they create a coordinated support system. Children can then practise managing challenge, recover from setbacks and begin to trust their own ability to adapt. Resilience also strengthens when adults use flexible thinking, support emotional literacy and make sure every child feels included and valued. These practices help children manage daily demands and build the foundation for learning and wellbeing.

As the programme moves into Unit 3, the focus shifts from understanding resilience to embedding it across the whole setting. The next unit demonstrates how these principles can be built into routines, systems and adult behaviours so that resilience is not the responsibility of one adult member. Instead, it becomes part of the culture of the setting and is reinforced consistently throughout the day. This whole-setting approach ensures that resilience is not only taught but actively lived and maintained over time.

Unit 3
Building a Whole-Setting Approach to Resilience

What this unit covers:

- Learn how a whole-setting approach builds resilience through safe relationships, predictable routines and consistent adult responses.
- Explore how education settings, families and communities work together to strengthen belonging, wellbeing and coping skills.
- Use practical strategies and tools to assess, embed and review resilience, including frameworks such as CYRM, WEMWBS and 5-A-Day for Wellbeing.

Introduction

Resilience develops not through dramatic moments or single lessons but through the small, everyday actions that help children feel safe, understood and valued. Research consistently shows that warm, attuned and predictable adult relationships are central to building resilience, particularly when children experience stress or adversity (Masten, 2014; Ungar, 2015). When adults respond calmly, keep routines predictable and take time to listen, they learn that the world is manageable and that they are capable of facing challenges. This is consistent with attachment theory, which demonstrates that secure and responsive caregiving underpins children's emotional regulation and confidence (Bowlby, 1988; Sroufe, 2005).

A whole-setting approach to resilience begins with a simple belief that every adult a child meets, whether they be teachers, office staff, lunchtime supervisors, parents, community members, all play a part in their emotional development. Evidence shows that resilience is strengthened through multiple protective relationships across a child's environment rather than through single interventions (Bronfenbrenner, 2005). Therefore, resilience becomes a shared responsibility rather than an isolated task and as a result children thrive when the messages they receive from their education setting, home and community all point in the same direction: you matter, you belong and you can cope with life's ups and downs. Studies emphasise that consistent support across settings has a cumulative effect on wellbeing and coping skills (Daniel and Wassell, 2002).

DOI: 10.4324/9781003409632-4

This unit focuses on what a whole-setting approach looks like in practice, by exploring how education settings can build a culture where children feel supported, how families can reinforce positive habits at home and how communities can contribute to a wider sense of belonging. It also looks at common barriers and offers practical strategies that adults can use straightaway. This reflects the growing evidence that resilience is best understood as a systemic process shaped by interactions between individuals and their environments (Masten and Barnes, 2018; Ungar, 2012).

The aim is to help create a way of working that becomes part of the education setting's identity, because when resilience is merged through daily routines, language and relationships it stops being something we teach and becomes something we live. Research shows that embedding relational, trauma-informed and resilience practices within daily life leads to meaningful and sustainable improvements in children's wellbeing, behaviour and engagement (Coburn and Gormally, 2017; Darling-Hammond et al., 2019).

Importance of a Whole-Setting Approach

Children learn best when they experience emotional safety created through predictable routines, consistent messages and adults who relate to them in a calm and attuned way. When children enter an environment where expectations are clear and relationships are warm, their bodies and minds relax enough to learn. Research in educational neuroscience shows that emotionally safe environments reduce the activation of the stress response system, allowing them to access the parts of the brain associated with reasoning, problem-solving and learning (Immordino-Yang and Damasio, 2007). They feel less anxious, less defensive and less overwhelmed, which gives them the mental space, the encouragement and the emotional support they need to try, to fail and to try again (Ungar 2012).

A whole-setting approach strengthens the connection between emotional wellbeing and learning. When children believe that they can cope with difficulty they become more engaged learners. They persevere for longer, they take risks in their learning and they are more open to feedback. Studies demonstrate that when settings embed wellbeing as part of their ethos, improvements in behaviour, attendance and academic outcomes often follow (Durlak et al., 2011). These improvements do not occur because the academic content has changed but because the emotional conditions for learning are stronger. Children feel confident enough to participate and brave enough to make mistakes.

Consistency plays a crucial role. When adults across the education setting speak to children using similar language and approaches, the environment becomes more predictable because they know how adults will respond. They understand that challenges can be met with problem-solving rather than reprimand. Predictability reduces anxiety and strengthens trust, particularly for those who have experienced adversity (Shonkoff et al., 2012). It also supports them in internalising positive messages about themselves as they begin to understand that mistakes are part of learning, that emotions can be managed and that asking for help is a sign of strength.

Belonging is another essential pillar of resilience. When children feel part of a community that notices them, includes them and celebrates their strengths, they feel grounded and secure. Research consistently links a sense of belonging within educational settings to improved wellbeing, higher engagement and stronger academic outcomes (Allen et al., 2018). This feeling of being valued helps children cope with setbacks, because they know they matter. However, belonging is not created through words on walls or slogans in assemblies and gatherings. It is built through everyday interactions, an adult greeting a child by name, a parent receiving a warm welcome at the gate, or a young person being supported to repair a relationship with a friend. Over time, these small moments accumulate into a culture where children genuinely feel that they belong.

A whole-setting approach matters because it brings together the different elements of children's lives into a coherent support system. When settings, families and communities align in their messages and approaches, children receive consistent reinforcement that they are supported, capable and resilient.

The Shared Role of Education Settings, Parents and Communities

Children's resilience develops most strongly when the key systems around them work together rather than in isolation. Education settings, families and communities each play a distinct yet interconnected role in creating the relational, emotional and environmental conditions that enable them to cope, adapt and thrive.

Education Settings as Foundations for Resilience

Education settings provide the structure and relationships that children rely on each day. Predictability, warmth and positive expectations create the foundation on which resilience can grow. Research consistently shows that secure, supportive relationships with adults are among the strongest predictors of resilience (Masten, 2014). When routines are clear and adults respond consistently, children feel secure. They are more able to explore, take risks and manage frustration when they trust the adults around them.

Embedding resilience into daily practice involves merging social and emotional learning throughout the curriculum, rather than treating it as an isolated activity. When this happens, classrooms become places where emotions can be talked about safely, mistakes are understood as part of learning and children are encouraged to think creatively and engage in problem-solving. A culture that prioritises persistence over perfection enables them to experience success through effort and strengthens their sense of personal agency, aligning with research on growth mindset and academic resilience (Dweck, 2017; Martin and Marsh, 2009).

Leadership is vital in sustaining this approach, therefore senior leaders set the emotional tone and prioritise wellbeing across the whole setting. Research shows that whole-setting approaches are most effective when leaders embed wellbeing into policy, staff development and everyday practice (Weare and Nind, 2011). When leaders model reflective thinking and relational behaviour, adults and children follow their example, reinforcing a culture of psychological safety and collective value (Leithwood et al., 2020).

Parents as Co-Educators

Families are central to a child's emotional development. Parental warmth, consistent boundaries and positive communication are powerful protective factors for mental health and resilience. When parents understand the aims of resilience-focused practice they are better placed to reinforce the same messages at home. Strong partnerships between education settings and home rely on open communication, shared understanding and trust, which reflects well-evidenced principles of effective home-school collaboration (Goodall and Montgomery, 2014).

Providing parents with practical information about wellbeing, for example supporting routines, managing anxiety or promoting balanced technology use, helps strengthen this partnership. Evidence suggests that when parents receive guidance and feel confident in their role, children's emotional and behavioural outcomes improve (Department for Education, 2018). Opportunities for families to participate in wellbeing events, community projects or celebration days build connection and increase confidence in supporting their child.

Recognising and valuing the diverse strengths that exist within families reinforces the understanding that every parent has a meaningful role in supporting their child's resilience. This strengths-based approach shifts the focus away from seen shortfalls and towards shared capability and partnership (Brooks, 2006; Ungar, 2012). When parents are positioned as co-educators rather than recipients of direction from education settings, collaboration becomes purposeful and consistent, creating continuity between home and setting. Morgan (2017) emphasises that learning, behaviour and wellbeing are most effectively supported when families and settings work in partnership, strengthened by shared language, expectations and goals. When children experience this partnership, evidence shows they feel more secure, supported and engaged (Epstein, 2011).

Communities as Networks of Support

A sense of community belonging strengthens resilience by helping children recognise that support extends beyond their home and education setting. Community level protective factors including safe environments, positive role models and opportunities for meaningful participation further enhance their capacity to cope with challenges (Bronfenbrenner, 2005; Luthar et al., 2015). Partnerships with local organisations, youth services, sports clubs, charities and health teams widen the circle of care around children, creating a broader, more connected network of support.

Community collaboration might involve mentoring opportunities, shared wellbeing initiatives or joint campaigns that promote positive mental health. Research shows that community engagement and extracurricular involvement promote confidence, belonging and social competence (Eccles and Gootman, 2002). Social action projects enable children to contribute meaningfully to their communities, building confidence, purpose and responsibility. These experiences strengthen protective factors by helping them see themselves as valued members of something bigger (Scales et al., 2016).

When education settings, families and communities work together, they create an integrated support system that reinforces resilience in multiple areas. This collective effort sends a clear message to them that they are not alone and they have people around them who want to help them succeed.

Overcoming Barriers

Despite strong intentions, education settings may encounter obstacles when embedding resilience-focused practice. Common barriers include:

- Curriculum pressure: When academic demands dominate, social and emotional development can be sidelined. Therefore, integrating resilience into core subjects ensures emotional learning remains a priority.
- Adult stress and workload: Adults cannot model resilience if their own wellbeing is compromised, so structured support, supervision and realistic expectations are essential.
- Fragmented approaches: Inconsistent practice weakens impact, so shared language, collaborative planning and whole-setting routines ensure consistency.
- Limited parental engagement: Families may feel unsure of how to contribute, therefore clear, welcoming communication and celebrating small steps forward help to build confidence.
- Resource constraints: Many resilience-building strategies rely on relationships and existing structures rather than additional funding. Creative use of peer support, cross-curricular links and child leadership can have significant impact.

Practical Strategies for Educators

Building resilience is most effective when it is intentionally included into leadership decisions, teaching practice and the wider culture of the setting. The strategies below provide practical, achievable approaches that support adults to create emotionally supportive environments where resilience can develop day by day.

LEADERSHIP COMMITMENT

Focus: Senior leaders shape the emotional culture of the education setting, therefore a clear commitment to resilience at leadership level communicates that wellbeing is central to effective teaching and learning.

Practical Application: This commitment is strengthened when strategic plans explicitly prioritise emotional development, policies are written using relational and inclusive language, and adult induction and continuing professional development consistently highlight wellbeing.

Reflection: Creating regular reflective spaces where they can consider workload, emotional demands and stress further reinforces this commitment. Appointing a resilience or wellbeing lead can support consistency and maintain momentum, while leadership that models empathy, authenticity and reflective practice encourages the whole community to represent these values in everyday interactions.

CURRICULUM INTEGRATION

Focus: Resilience is strengthened when children are able to explore emotions, identity and challenge across a range of subjects.

Practical Application: Opportunities can be built into the curriculum through discussing characters' responses to difficulty in English and drama, examining the science of stress and self-regulation, connecting physical activity with mental health in PE and using creative subjects to express and reflect on feelings. Social and emotional learning frameworks provide the structure and consistency needed to weave these themes throughout the organisation.

Reflection: The overall aim is to normalise conversations about emotions and to help children understand how resilience connects to their everyday learning.

STAFF DEVELOPMENT AND MODELLING

Focus: Children's understanding of resilience is shaped significantly by the adults they observe.

Practical Application: Regular professional development on topics such as trauma-informed practice, attachment theory and emotional coaching enables adults to respond with greater confidence. Peer mentoring, shared problem solving and recognition of relational practice help build a supportive culture, reinforcing that emotional wellbeing is everyone's responsibility.

Reflection: When adults respond to pressure with reflection rather than reactivity they learn valuable lessons about emotional regulation.

ENVIRONMENT AND ETHOS

Focus: A calm, welcoming environment sends powerful messages that children are valued and safe.

Practical Application: Displays that celebrate effort, creativity and community connections reinforce a culture where growth and perseverance are recognised. Restorative approaches to conflict help them learn that relationships can be repaired through dialogue and understanding. Routine practices such as calm starts to the day or checking in with them strengthens connection and prepares them for learning.

Reflection: When the environment reflects the emotional values of the setting it creates a lived experience of resilience.

FAMILY AND COMMUNITY PARTNERSHIP

Focus: Regular, planned communication with families helps create a shared understanding of resilience.

Practical Application: This can include newsletters offering practical wellbeing tips, family challenges designed to encourage curiosity, effort and bravery such as those found in Morgan's Family Growth Mindset Scheme Pack (Morgan, n.d.) and community assemblies that highlight local examples of perseverance. Collaborative initiatives involving parents, children and community partners demonstrate that wellbeing is a collective priority.

Reflection: When children and experience consistent language and support across their home, setting and community environments, resilience becomes reinforced in ways that feel natural, meaningful and continuous.

Assessing Resilience

Before we can meaningfully support a child to develop their resilience, we must first understand their starting point. A structured assessment process provides a clear picture of where they are now and what they need in order to move forward. Research consistently shows that resilience develops through a dynamic interaction between internal attributes and external protective factors (Ungar, 2012). Without an assessment framework, decisions risk being based on assumptions rather than grounded in evidence.

Two well-established tools that enable education settings and adults to identify strengths, vulnerabilities and the wider environmental influences on children's wellbeing and behaviour are the Child and Youth Resilience Measure (CYRM) and the Warwick-Edinburgh Mental Wellbeing Scale (WEMWBS).

The Child and Youth Resilience Measure (CYRM)

The Child and Youth Resilience Measure (CYRM), developed by Dr Michael Ungar and the Resilience Research Centre in Canada, offers a clear way to understand the individual, family and community factors that shape a child's resilience. Reflecting international research, the CYRM recognises that resilience grows not only from personal strengths but from the quality of the support surrounding the child.

The measure is widely used in education settings and can be completed one to one, particularly with younger children, in around 20 minutes. The shorter CYRM-12 provides a more accessible option, scoring highlights both strengths and environmental needs, helping adults plan support that strengthens belonging, connection and consistency. The CYRM is free for educational and research use (permission via the Resilience Research Centre).

The CYRM-28 is designed for use across a broad developmental range, with a child version for ages 5-9 and a youth version for ages 10-23, and can be completed either as a self-report or with adult assistance where appropriate. It assesses three interconnected domains of resilience: individual capacities and resources such as problem solving and peer support, relationships with primary caregivers including trust and family cohesion, and contextual factors such as cultural identity, sense of belonging and community safety. Together, these domains provide a holistic picture of the protective factors supporting a child's resilience and highlight areas where further development may be beneficial.

The Warwick-Edinburgh Mental Wellbeing Scale (WEMWBS)

The Warwick-Edinburgh Mental Wellbeing Scale (WEMWBS), developed by the Universities of Warwick and Edinburgh, offers a clear and accessible way to understand how young people feel and function in their everyday lives. Using positively framed statements such as feeling optimistic about the future or feeling close to others, the scale records key aspects of mental wellbeing through either a 14 item or shorter 7 item version. This emphasis on everyday experience makes WEMWBS particularly relevant for education and youth settings, where subtle shifts in confidence, connection and mood can have a meaningful impact on engagement, behaviour and learning.

WEMWBS is widely used as an outcome measure and is especially helpful for tracking change following resilience or wellbeing-focused interventions. It is well validated, straightforward to administer and free for non-commercial use, making it a practical choice for settings. The scale is suitable for young people aged 13 and over, with adapted versions available for younger children. However, while WEMWBS provides a valuable snapshot of overall wellbeing, it does not explain why difficulties may be present. For this reason, it is most effective when used alongside other tools such as the Strengths and Difficulties Questionnaire (SDQ), Child and Youth Resilience Measure and professional judgement to build a fuller and deeper understanding of a child's needs.

Building a Focused, Whole-Setting Approach to Developing Resilience

Once an initial assessment has been completed using tools such as the CYRM or WEMWBS, the next step is to use this information to shape everyday practice across the setting. Assessment offers a clear starting point it identifies the aspects of resilience that are already secure and highlights those that require further attention. This enables adults to target their work more effectively rather than relying on assumptions. However lasting improvement comes from what happens consistently from what children see, hear and practise day after day.

A practical way to achieve this consistency is to establish a monthly focus on resilience across the whole setting. For younger children the monthly theme can be broken down into weekly strands, while older children can work directly with a monthly focus, for example choosing observable behaviours such as "We keep going when work feels challenging", "We break big tasks into smaller steps", "We stay calm when plans change", or "We make choices that help us and others feel safe" helps them recognise what resilience looks and feels like in action. Adults can then intentionally notice and celebrate these behaviours, reinforcing a positive and predictable culture.

Embedding resilience within routines, shared language and everyday interactions ensures that these skills are practised rather than merely taught. Children receive immediate reinforcement from adults and can apply their learning across a variety of contexts.

Another effective way to structure this whole-setting focus is through the Resilience Framework for Children and Young People, developed by Boingboing.org.uk (Boingboing, n.d.). The framework's five domains, Basics, Belonging, Learning, Coping and Core Self which provide a clear, strengths-based map for selecting weekly or monthly themes. As the framework is visual and designed for collaborative use, adults and children can work together to select focus areas that align with assessment findings as well as the setting's contextual needs. Elements such as understanding feelings, feeling safe, having a trusted adult or managing everyday stress can then be included into routines and conversations, ensuring resilience is developed systemically rather than reactively.

Specific Interventions Promoting Resilience

When embedded within a whole-education approach, specific interventions can offer a structured and effective way to strengthen resilience in children and the adults who support them. These programmes typically draw on evidence from psychology, education and public health and are designed to build core skills such as emotional literacy, cognitive flexibility, self-regulation, problem solving and confidence.

While each intervention varies in focus and delivery, they are most impactful when they align with the setting's values, priorities and identified needs, when adults receive appropriate training, guidance and ongoing support, when delivery is consistent, inclusive and sustained over time and when everyday practice reinforces and models the skills being taught. Used consistently, resilience-building programmes contribute to a wider culture of care, enabling settings to respond proactively to the challenges that children and families may face. The aim is not to offer a quick fix but to strengthen long-term protective factors that support wellbeing, engagement and readiness to learn. One such example is the 5-A-Day for Wellbeing Model, which illustrates how evidence-based principles can be translated into everyday practice in ways that are accessible, sustainable and meaningful across a whole education community.

Structured Frameworks: The 5-A-Day for Wellbeing Model

The 5-A-Day for Wellbeing framework developed by NHS Greater Glasgow & Clyde (n.d.), provides a practical and evidence-based model for promoting resilience and emotional wellbeing across schools, workplaces and communities. Adapted from the Five Ways to Wellbeing model developed by the New Economics Foundation (NEF, 2008), it translates the science of positive mental health into accessible, everyday actions that can be embedded into organisational culture.

Grounded in public-health and positive-psychology research, the 5-A-Day model encourages individuals and communities to take proactive steps to maintain mental health and resilience. In an educational setting, this framework supports a whole approach by aligning adult wellbeing, child development and community engagement around the same five principles, Contribute, Be Healthy, Accept, Connect and Be Aware of Your Feelings.

1. **Contribute**
   Resilience research consistently highlights the protective role of selflessness, purpose and contribution. Helping others activates a sense of belonging and self-efficacy both of which are central to psychological resilience (Post, 2005). Encouraging children and adults to get involved with causes they care about, use their talents to support others and offer help within the community cultivates empathy, cooperation and meaning. Settings can put this into practice by integrating volunteering, peer-mentoring and child voice initiatives into their culture, reinforcing the belief that everyone has something valuable to contribute.
2. **Be Healthy**
   Physical health is a cornerstone of emotional resilience; research demonstrates strong links between physical activity, nutrition, sleep and mental wellbeing (Public Health England, 2019). The Be Healthy feature promotes daily physical activity, balanced diet, quality sleep and self-care, recognising that physiological wellbeing underpins children ability to self-regulate and cope with stress. Within a whole-setting approach, wellbeing policies can include active break initiatives, mindful movement, sleep education lessons and adults' modelling of healthy work–life balance.
3. **Accept**
   Self-acceptance and self-compassion are essential components of resilience, reducing vulnerability to anxiety, perfectionism and low self-esteem (Neff, 2011). The Accept element encourages children to acknowledge strengths and limitations, receive positive feedback and develop healthy self-esteem. Education settings can reinforce this by embedding a growth-mindset culture (Dweck, 2006), celebrating effort as well as achievement and supporting reflective conversations about identity and self-worth. By normalising imperfection and promoting self-kindness, the setting builds a psychologically safe environment in which both adults and children can thrive.
4. **Connect**
   Social connectedness is one of the strongest predictors of resilience and lifelong wellbeing (World Health Organization, 2020). The Connect component focuses on nurturing secure, supportive relationships encouraging individuals to stay close to family and friends, build positive community links and identify at least one trusted adult. In education settings, this aligns directly with attachment-informed practice and whole-setting belonging strategies. Creating opportunities for collaboration, restorative dialogue and mentoring strengthens the relational fabric of the setting community ensuring that children and adults alike feel valued and supported.
5. **Be Aware of Your Feelings**
   Emotional awareness and regulation are fundamental to resilience (Gross, 2015). The Be Aware of Your Feelings strand helps individuals to notice the connection between thoughts, feelings and behaviours, balance self-criticism with more constructive thinking and keep an open mind. Education settings can embed this through Social and Emotional Aspects of Learning (SEAL), mindfulness practice and

reflective check-ins that develop emotional literacy. This focus supports children to manage stress, reduce impulsive reactions and make more considered choices when under pressure.

Evaluation and Reflection

Evaluating a whole-setting approach to resilience involves noticing the difference it makes to how children and adults feel, behave and learn. A blend of quantitative and qualitative information provides a balanced view of progress. Attendance patterns, wellbeing measures, short surveys and brief case examples help settings understand how secure and connected children feel, while observations of relationships and classroom climate offer insight into the everyday experience of the setting.

Reflection is most effective when it forms part of regular practice, adult discussions give space to explore what is working well, where consistency needs strengthening and how children are responding to the culture around them. Helpful questions may include:

- Are adults modelling and reinforcing resilience in day-to-day interactions?
- Do children feel safe, included and valued across the setting?
- Do our policies and routines reflect our commitment to wellbeing and inclusion?
- What evidence shows improvements in belonging and emotional wellbeing?

Ongoing evaluation helps keep resilience included into everyday practice rather than treated as occasional, stand-alone behaviour. It allows settings to refine their approach and maintain a culture where children feel supported, capable and ready to learn.

Connecting the Learning

This unit has demonstrated that resilience is developed through everyday experiences rather than through isolated or short-term interventions. Predictable routines, calm and attuned adults and consistent messages across education settings, families and communities create the conditions in which children feel safe, valued and capable. When these conditions are present, children are better able to engage with learning, manage their emotions and recover from challenge. Resilience, therefore, is not something a child simply has or does not have; it is a dynamic, relational process shaped by the environments and relationships that surround them (Masten, 2014; Ungar, 2012).

A whole-setting approach supports this process by establishing shared language, consistent expectations and strong relational practice, helping children experience continuity rather than contradiction. Leadership plays a critical role in sustaining this culture. When wellbeing is prioritised at a strategic level and adults feel supported, they are more able to model the calm, predictable and reflective behaviours that underpin resilience for all (Weare and Nind, 2011; Leithwood et al., 2020).

Embedding resilience within routines, curriculum experiences and everyday interactions ensures that skills are practised regularly rather than taught in isolation. Ongoing reflection and evaluation, using tools such as the CYRM, WEMWBS and the Resilience Framework, enable settings to refine their approach and ensure resilience remains part of daily practice rather than a reactive response to difficulty.

While a whole-setting approach provides essential external protection, children also need opportunities to develop the internal skills required to navigate challenge independently. Safe, supportive environments lay the foundation, but resilience is strengthened further when children can recognise their emotions, understand their thinking and reflect on how these influence their behaviour. This connection between external support and internal capacity leads into Unit 4, which explores self-awareness as a core component of emotional intelligence and a key factor in enabling children to make full use of the supportive environments around them.

Unit 4
Developing Self-Awareness

What this unit covers:

- Recognise and name emotions, thoughts and behaviours to build self-awareness and resilience.
- Develop emotional vocabulary, body awareness and insight into triggers and patterns.
- Complete practical reflection and creative tasks such as feelings check-ins, thought-feeling-action chains, journalling and strength spotting.

Introduction

This unit explores how self-awareness strengthens resilience by helping children understand their own emotions, thoughts and behaviours. It examines self-awareness as the foundation of emotional intelligence (Goleman, 1995) and a key factor in developing control, confidence and adaptability when faced with challenges. Drawing on research from social and emotional learning frameworks (Collaborative for Academic, Social and Emotional Learning (CASEL), 2020), the unit explains how understanding internal states supports emotional regulation, positive relationships and decision making (Durlak et al., 2011). Practical strategies and activities that promote self-awareness are also introduced, including emotional vocabulary development, reflection, body awareness and strength- spotting to help them build insight, confidence and resilience in everyday life.

In developing self-awareness, this unit recognises the importance of giving children safe, structured opportunities to pause, notice and name their internal experiences, a process supported by research showing that naming emotions supports regulation (Siegel, 2012). Many find it difficult to articulate what they are feeling until emotions have become overwhelming, leading to behaviours that mask rather than express their needs. By approaching self-awareness as a teachable skill rather than an assumed ability, adults can support them to develop a clearer understanding of what is happening inside them and why. This deliberate, guided attention to thoughts, feelings and physical cues helps explain emotional experiences (Denham, Bassett and Wyatt, 2012) and fosters a sense of control that is essential

DOI: 10.4324/9781003409632-5

for resilience. When embedded consistently across learning environments, self-awareness empowers them not only to understand themselves more deeply but also to communicate their needs with greater clarity, strengthening relationships with friends, adults and families.

Importance of Self-Awareness

Self-awareness is a fundamental building block of emotional intelligence and a core component in the development of resilience, enabling children to recognise their own emotions, thoughts and behaviours and understand how these influence their actions and relationships. When they are self-aware, they are better equipped to make positive choices, manage stress and respond to challenges with greater control and confidence.

Research conducted by the Collaborative for Academic, Social and Emotional Learning (Collaborative for Academic, Social and Emotional Learning [CASEL], 2020) identified self-awareness as one of the five key competencies for social and emotional learning, defining it as the ability to accurately recognise one's own emotions, thoughts, strengths and limitations and to develop a well grounded sense of confidence and optimism. Further studies show that children with higher levels of self-awareness demonstrate improved emotional regulation and impulse control (Denham, Bassett and Wyatt, 2012), stronger relationships with peers and adults (Collaborative for Academic, Social and Emotional Learning [CASEL], 2020), greater academic success (Durlak et al., 2011) and increased resilience when facing setbacks or emotional challenges (Reivich and Shatté, 2002). Developing self-awareness helps them to understand why they react in certain ways and to recognise the physical and emotional signals that occur when they are stressed, frustrated or upset. Once these internal cues can be identified, they are able to make more conscious decisions about how to respond.

Self-Awareness Builds Resilience

Resilience is not about avoiding difficult situations it is about navigating them with understanding and adaptability. Children who are self-aware can recognise when they are feeling anxious, angry or overwhelmed and are therefore better able to apply coping strategies or ask for help. Without self-awareness emotions can take control, leading to impulsive reactions or withdrawal. For example, a child who is aware that they feel tense and irritable before a test can use breathing techniques, positive self-talk or physical movement to calm themselves. By identifying the trigger and recognising their emotional state, they can take action rather than being overwhelmed by it.

Bandura's (1997) theory of self-efficacy highlights that a strong sense of self-awareness allows individuals to notice their progress and build confidence through mastery experiences. When they understand their emotions and how they respond to pressure, they become more capable of managing it. Over time, this strengthens their belief that they can influence outcomes through their own effort and regulation a central feature of resilience.

When teaching resilience, it is therefore essential to begin with self-awareness, helping them to tune into their emotional and physical signals, understand their strengths and identify areas where they can grow.

Strategies to Develop Self-Awareness

The following activities last between 20 and 40 minutes and are designed for children aged 7 to 14, with adaptations made as needed for younger or older children. Each activity is structured under the following headings, Purpose, Instructions, Discussion Prompts, and Extension or Adaptation. It is important to maintain emotional safety by ensuring that all contributions are respected and valued and by reinforcing that resilience grows through experience and reflection rather than through perfection.

Activity: Feelings Thermometer

Purpose

This activity helps children and young people build emotional awareness by noticing how their feelings rise and fall throughout the day. By tuning into these internal changes, they begin to understand what influences their emotions and how to use simple strategies to stay steady, connected and ready to learn.

Instructions

Begin by explaining that all of us experience a full spectrum of feelings each day and that none of these are good or bad. What matters is recognising them and knowing what helps us cope. Create a large 'feelings thermometer' on a board or flipchart, dividing it into five coloured sections that illustrate increasing emotional intensity:

1. Calm (blue)
2. Settled (green)
3. Uneasy (yellow)
4. Frustrated (orange)
5. Overwhelmed (red)

Add simple words or symbols to support children who benefit from visual prompts and give each a name card, photograph or familiar token. At the start or end of the day along with key transition points such as arrival, after playtime or following a challenging activity invite them to place their token at the level that best represents how they feel. Model this to normalise honest check-ins. Encourage brief reflection "What made you feel this way today?" "Has anything changed since you last checked in?" Provide reassurance that feelings change and that noticing these changes is a strength. As a group generate a list of strategies that help when emotions intensify, such as breathing techniques, grounding activities, movement breaks or speaking with a trusted adult. Revisit the thermometer throughout the week to help children spot patterns, feel validated and develop confidence in managing their emotional landscape.

Discussion Prompts

Use these prompts to help them talk about noticing their feelings, managing them and supporting others.

- How can we tell when our feelings are getting bigger?
- How does knowing our feelings help us make good choices?
- What helps us when our feelings start to feel too big?
- How can we be kind to someone whose feelings are higher on the thermometer?
- What helps us feel calm again?

Extension or Adaptation Options

Use a three-step thermometer for younger children or for those who benefit from simpler visuals, helping them recognise calm, in-between and big feelings. Older children may enjoy keeping a short reflection journal or using digital check-ins to track their feelings over time. Families can also create a home version of the thermometer to encourage shared conversations about emotions and routines. In one-to-one or alternative provision settings, personalise the scale with them, adding their own words, colours or symbols and co-develop calming strategies that feel meaningful to them.

Activity: Feelings Thermometer

Purpose

This activity helps children to recognise, name and describe their emotions with greater clarity. Developing a rich emotional vocabulary strengthens self-awareness, self-regulation, empathy and confident communication. Through the use of visual tools and structured reflection, children learn that noticing and identifying emotions early allows them to understand their internal signals and make choices that build resilience in everyday situations.

Instructions

Begin by introducing the idea that everyone experiences a wide range of emotions and that naming these feelings can make them easier to manage. Display a simple visual prompt such as a feelings wheel or emotion chart and invite them to identify emotions they already recognise, grouping them into broad categories for example, happy, sad, angry, worried, excited, to build a shared language. Provide each with an emotion card and ask them to choose one emotion to explore. Model this first by sharing a brief example of a time a particular emotion was felt, what was noticed in the body and what helped with coping. Then encourage them to offer short reflections of their own.

Introduce a Feelings Thermometer by explaining that emotions rise and fall in intensity, much like temperature. Show how the lower end of the thermometer represents calm or settled feelings, while the upper end reflects emotions that may feel overwhelming. Provide blank templates for them to personalise with emotion words, physical signs such as tense shoulders or butterflies in the stomach and strategies that help them return to a steadier state. Establish a simple check-in routine by inviting them to select an emotion word or place a name token on the thermometer to show how they feel in that moment. Revisit the thermometer at the end of the session to highlight how emotions naturally shift throughout the day.

Discussion Prompts

Use these questions to help them think about their feelings, how feelings show up in their bodies and how understanding emotions can help them make good choices and support others.

- Why is it helpful to have words for our feelings?
- How does your body let you know when a feeling is getting bigger?
- What helps you when your feelings start building up?
- How could understanding feelings help you make good choices or help someone else?

Extension or Adaptation Options

For younger children use puppets, emojis or simple images to help them recognise and name emotions in an accessible way. Older children can be supported to explore a wider range of feeling words, adding personalised statements or examples to their emotion thermometers to deepen understanding. In one-to-one sessions, consider creating an individual emotion dictionary or a resilient response plan linked to the different thermometer levels to help them recognise early signs and choose helpful actions. Families can also be encouraged to use shared emotion charts at home so that they experience consistent language and expectations across education and home settings.

Activity: My Body, My Feelings

Purpose

This activity supports children to develop self-awareness by noticing how their body responds to different emotional states. Understanding early physical signs of stress, calm or frustration helps them recognise what is happening for them internally and strengthens their capacity to regulate under pressure.

Instructions

Begin by creating a quiet, settled atmosphere and invite them to sit or stand comfortably and explain that the activity is about gently noticing what is happening in their body, without needing to change anything. Reinforce that bodies give us clues when emotions are building and learning to notice these signals is a key resilience skill. Guide them into a simple breathing focus and ask them to place one hand on their stomach and one on their chest. Encourage slow breaths in through the nose and out through the mouth, noticing each rise and fall. Allow a few cycles of breathing so they can observe any shifts in tension or calm.

Move into a body scan and guide attention to specific areas for example "Notice your feet on the floor . . . your legs . . . your shoulders . . . your face." Encourage them to observe sensations such as tightness, warmth, heaviness or ease.

Introduce gentle stretch and release movements and invite them to reach their arms upwards, roll their shoulders or softly shake out their hands. Frame these actions as ways to release built up tension and create space for more helpful emotional responses. Finish with reflection and ask them to share verbally or in writing what they noticed. Reinforce that recognising physical signs is the first step in responding to emotional pressure with greater choice and control.

Discussion Prompts

Use these questions to help them think about how their bodies feel in different moments and how noticing those feelings can make tricky times easier to handle.

- What clues does your body give you when you start to feel worried or stressed?
- How does your body feel when you are calm, relaxed or happy?
- Which part of today's activity helped your body feel the most relaxed?
- How could listening to your body help you when something feels difficult at your setting, at home or with friends?

Extension or Adaptation Options

Younger children may respond well to a story-based body scan, guided through noticing different parts of the body using simple, imaginative language. Older children can begin to link physical sensations to emotional triggers. Visual body outlines can support those who benefit from something concrete to look at or draw on when describing how their body feels. In one-to-one work, this activity can be paired with emotion coaching to support children to identify feelings and choose helpful responses. Families can be encouraged to use a short calming stretch or breathing routine at home, allowing children to experience the same strategies in different settings and build confidence and consistency over time.

Activity: The Inside Outside Me

Purpose

This activity supports children to build self-awareness by exploring the difference between what is felt internally and what is shown externally, they gain insight into how emotions influence behaviour, choices and communication. The activity normalises all feelings and encourages thoughtful responses rather than automatic reactions, helping those involved develop healthier emotional expression and greater control under pressure.

Instructions

Create a calm space where they can think quietly and speak without interruption. Introduce the idea that people often feel one thing inside but show something different on the outside. Offer simple, everyday examples such as, laughing when embarrassed or withdrawing when overwhelmed to help them connect with the concept. Provide each with a blank page or an outline labelled inside and outside. Explain that the inside represents thoughts and feelings, while the outside reflects actions, expressions or body language. Invite them to fill in each section using words, sketches or symbols that show how they might feel internally and how they might behave outwardly in various situations. Emphasise that this is a private reflection; there are no right or wrong responses.

Once complete, invite them to look at both sections and notice any differences between their inner and outer experiences. Facilitate a discussion about what these differences might represent. Reinforce the idea that recognising emotions creates choice, when what is happening internally is understood, their responses can be more intentional and supportive.

Discussion Prompts

Use these questions to help them explore the difference between what they feel on the inside and what they show on the outside and how this can help them deal with big emotions and get along with others.

- Can you think of a time when you felt one thing on the inside but showed something different on the outside?
- Why do you think you acted or spoke that way, at the time?
- How could noticing the difference between your inside feelings and your outside actions help you with big feelings?
- What might happen if you ignore your inside feelings for a long time?
- How could understanding your inside outside self, help you get on better with friends, family or people at your setting?

Extension or Adaptation Options

For younger children use emotion symbols, colour zones or simple drawings to help them show the difference between their inside and outside feelings. For older children encourage them to write about a real situation where their inside and outside feelings were different. Ask them to think about what helped them cope at the time and what they might try next time they have big emotions. In group settings create a shared resilient responses wall where everyone adds ideas, pictures or examples of positive strategies they use when feelings get big. Invite a parent or trusted adult to complete an Inside outside me sheet alongside their child. This can strengthen communication, build empathy and help both adult and child understand each other's feelings and reactions on a deeper level.

Activity: Learning From My Choices

Purpose

This activity supports children to develop emotional literacy, self-awareness and the ability to notice how their feelings influence their actions. Regular reflection strengthens the foundations of resilience by helping them recognise patterns, manage emotional shifts and draw on strategies that support them during challenge or change.

Instructions

Introduce the idea that reflection is a simple, honest pause to understand what is happening inside us and how this affects what we do. Use clear, age-appropriate language and model the process, for example "I realised I felt tense this morning, so I took a few deep breaths before joining the group. It helped me feel settled." Provide journals or reflection sheets and offer structured sentence starters such as "Today I felt . . .", "Something that stretched me today was . . .", "I noticed I reacted when . . .", "Next time, I could try . . .". Encourage them to work quietly for five to ten minutes, emphasising that there are no correct answers. The aim is to notice, not to judge.

If suitable, invite them to share one reflection in pairs or small groups. Establish expectations around listening, respect and choice reminding them that keeping reflections private is always acceptable. Finish the activity by highlighting key messages, reflection helps us understand our experiences, see small steps of progress and prepare ourselves with more effective coping strategies in the future. Reinforce that these skills are central to resilient thinking and behaviour.

Discussion Prompts

Use these questions to help them think about their feelings, notice what helps them cope and understand how looking back on their experiences can guide them in the future.

- What helps you notice when your feelings start to change?
- Did talking or writing about what happened make it feel any different afterwards?
- Can you think of a time when you managed a situation better than you expected?
- Have you noticed anything that often makes things feel tricky, or anything that helps you feel better again?
- How might thinking about what has happened before help you make good choices next time?

Extension or Adaptation Options

For younger children, use drawings, symbols or emoji-based reflection sheets and for older children introduce simple weekly summaries where they reflect on their goals, what went well and what they want to work on next. In one-to-one sessions these reflections can be used to guide targeted pastoral or emotional support. Adults can look for patterns, strengths and areas where they may need extra help or encouragement. In group settings consider creating an anonymous growth wall where they can add notes, drawings or examples of insights and achievements. This encourages a positive, supportive atmosphere and helps everyone see that growth looks different for each person.

Activity: The Thought, Feeling, Action Chain

Purpose

This activity introduces children to the connection between what they think, how they feel and the choices they make. By making this chain clear and visible, children begin to recognise that while they cannot always control what happens, they can influence how they respond internally. The activity builds emotional literacy and supports the development of self-regulation skills.

Instructions

Begin by explaining that our thoughts, feelings and actions are connected. Invite the group to consider the question "When something challenging happens, which comes first?" Draw three connected shapes on the board labelled thought, feeling and action to establish the chain visually. Use a simple example, such as "If I think, 'Everyone will laugh at me', I might feel embarrassed and choose to stay quiet. But if I think, 'I can give it a try', I might feel more confident and speak up." Provide each with a blank thought, feeling, action template and a scenario or prompt. Ask them to complete each part of the chain "What might they think in this situation?" "How could that thought make them feel?" "What action might follow?"

Once the first chain is complete, ask them to focus on changing only the thought. Encourage alternatives that are balanced and focused, such as "I can have another go" or "I'm still learning this." Guide them to re-complete the feeling and action sections, noticing how a shift in thinking influences the rest of the chain. Reinforce that thoughts are internal messages that can be explored and reshaped to support more resilient responses.

Discussion Prompts

Use these questions to help them notice how their thoughts, feelings and actions are linked and how changing a thought can make tough moments easier to manage.

- Which part was easiest for you to notice, your thought, your feeling or your action?
- Which part was trickiest to spot?
- What happened when you changed the thought? Did it change how you felt or what you did?
- Can you remember a real time when you used a more helpful thought?
- How could this idea help you if you're having friendship worries, make a mistake or find your work difficult?

Extension or Adaptation Options

Adapt the activity by using visual supports such as emojis, colour cues or simple story-based scenarios to help children understand the links between thoughts, feelings and actions. Younger children may find it helpful to match pictures to each part of the chain or act out short examples. Older children can apply the chain to more complex situations such as academic pressure, friendship worries or social conflict, allowing them to practise using more helpful thoughts in real life contexts. In one-to-one sessions, take time to explore personal examples in greater depth so they can recognise their own patterns and rehearse alternative responses. A blank chain can also be shared at home to encourage families to talk together about tricky moments and practise reflective, resilient thinking as a team.

Activity: Strength Spotting

Purpose

To help children recognise, articulate and build upon their personal strengths through the experience of giving and receiving constructive feedback. By nurturing a culture where strengths are named and effort is valued, they develop confidence, self-awareness and the resilient mindset needed to manage challenge and change.

Instructions

Create simple strength-spotting cards or sheets showing a broad range of character strengths, for example, perseverance, kindness, curiosity, teamwork, creativity. Alongside these, display a feedback framework that models clear, supportive language such as "I noticed . . .", "A strength you showed was . . ." and "Next time, you might try . . .". Provide pens, sticky notes and reflection journals. Begin by introducing the purpose of feedback and allow around ten minutes for discussion, inviting them to share what helpful feedback looks and feels like. Emphasise that constructive feedback is designed to notice strengths and guide growth, not to judge or criticise.

Model the process using a fictional example or shared piece of work and keep this demonstration focused and clear to identify a strength, explain why it matters and offer one realistic next step. Organise them into pairs or small groups and ask each to share a recent piece of work for example written, creative or practical. Using the framework, they identify at least two strengths and one suggestion for development. Move into their reflection by asking them to note down which feedback felt most helpful, which strengths they were able to recognise in themselves and how noticing these strengths could support them during challenging moments. Finish with a short group discussion to highlight key learning about resilience, confidence and the importance of feeling seen and valued.

Discussion Prompts

Use these questions to help them think about their strengths, how feedback feels and how these ideas can support them when things get tricky.

- How did it feel when someone pointed out a strength you didn't realise you had?
- What made some feedback feel really helpful? What made some feel less helpful?
- How could knowing your strengths help you when you're having a tough day?
- What do you think happens if we only focus on the things we find hard?
- Which ways of giving feedback helped you speak kindly and explain your ideas clearly?

Extension or Adaptation Options

For younger children, visual strength cards, symbols or stickers can be used to help them recognise and name their strengths in a concrete and engaging way. With older children, identified strengths can be linked to personal goals, leadership skills or future career aspirations to deepen their sense of purpose. Non-verbal options such as drawing, using symbols or completing digital templates can support those who communicate more comfortably in alternative ways. In one-to-one sessions, a personal strengths log can be created and revisited over time. Families can also be involved by creating a home feedback wall, where everyone shares examples of strengths, effort and kindness.

Connecting the Learning

As children develop greater self-awareness they begin to notice patterns in their emotions, thoughts and physical responses, alongside a growing understanding of their personal strengths. This awareness is not an end point; it is instead a vital foundation that makes meaningful resilience possible. When they can recognise what is happening inside them and why, they are better placed to respond with intention instead of reacting on impulse.

Throughout Unit 4, structured opportunities to build emotional vocabulary, tune in to bodily signals, reflect on experiences and explore the links between thoughts, feelings and actions have helped to demystify emotional experiences. These processes support children to make sense of themselves with greater clarity and confidence. They also create the conditions for emotional regulation. It is difficult to manage what you cannot first notice or name.

Adults play a central role in strengthening this learning. By modelling reflective language, naming emotions accurately, offering strengths-based feedback and creating predictable moments for emotional check-ins, they establish environments where self-awareness is practised consistently and safely. When this happens, children are more likely to communicate their needs, engage positively with others and draw on their strengths during challenge.

Unit 5 builds directly on this foundation by introducing practical strategies to regulate emotions, manage stress and regain balance in the moment. Together these units bridge the gap between recognising emotions and responding to them effectively, supporting the development of confident, adaptable resilience that can be applied across education settings, home and wider life contexts.

Unit 5

Emotional Regulation and Managing Stress

What this unit covers:

- Recognise emotions, identify triggers and early stress signals, and choose calm responses that support learning and relationships.
- Understand how stress affects the brain and body, and practise regulation strategies such as breathing, grounding, mindfulness and movement.
- Complete practical tasks including Safe Place and Calm Corner activities, plus tools like See It, Own It, Change It and circles of control to manage pressure.

Introduction

This unit explores emotional regulation and stress management as essential skills for resilience, wellbeing and positive relationships. It focuses on helping children recognise what they feel, understand why they feel it and choose helpful ways to respond when faced with challenge or pressure. Emotional regulation is not about suppressing emotions but about managing them effectively so that thinking and learning can continue, even in stressful moments (Siegel, 2012). Through practical strategies, reflective activities and supportive relationships, they learn to notice early signs of stress, calm their bodies and refocus their minds. When adults model calm, predictable responses and create safe, responsive environments, children develop the confidence to master the moment, building the self-awareness, control and resilience needed to thrive in learning and life (Shonkoff, 2020).

This work is most effective when it is rooted in a climate of trust and connection. Children learn how to regulate not simply through instruction but through the everyday experience of being understood, supported and guided by adults who respond with steadiness and empathy (National Scientific Council on the Developing Child, 2015). As seen across successful family education setting partnerships, emotional development strengthens when expectations are clear, routines are consistent and communication feels accessible and respectful. When children sense that the adults around them are working with them rather than directing at them, they become more open to exploring what helps them feel safe, what triggers stress and which strategies allow them to return to balance. Emotional

DOI: 10.4324/9781003409632-6

regulation is enhanced through predictable structures, calm modelling and the secure sense that no one is required to manage difficult feelings alone.

Importance of Emotional Regulation

Emotional regulation refers to the ability to understand and manage emotions effectively, especially in challenging situations. It involves recognising what we feel, understanding why we feel it and choosing an appropriate way to respond rather than react. This skill is fundamental to resilience, wellbeing and positive relationships for both children and adults.

Research from the Center on the Developing Child at Harvard University identifies responsive relationships as one of the most powerful protective factors against stress (Shonkoff, 2020). When individuals feel connected, supported and safe, their brains and bodies are better able to regulate emotional responses and recover from challenges more efficiently. When stress is chronic or unbuffered, it can disrupt brain development and have lasting effects on learning, behaviour and health.

Emotional regulation is not about suppressing or ignoring feelings but about managing them in healthy, adaptive ways. Siegel (2012) compares this process to surfing the wave, acknowledging emotions as they rise and fall without being overwhelmed by them. For children emotional regulation develops gradually through consistent modelling, practice and secure relationships. Adults who remain calm, predictable and emotionally available demonstrate to children that difficult emotions can be managed safely and effectively. When education settings and families work together to support emotional regulation, children are more likely to demonstrate improved focus and attention, develop empathy and social understanding, manage conflict and frustration more effectively, show higher levels of resilience and problem solving and experience better mental and physical health outcomes.

Managing Stress Builds Resilience

Stress management plays a central role in developing resilience, the ability to recover, adapt and grow stronger in response to challenge. While stress itself is a natural and unavoidable part of life, unmanaged or prolonged stress can negatively affect physical health, emotional stability and cognitive performance (McEwen, 2017). Helping children recognise and manage stress supports healthy brain function, emotional balance and sustained engagement in learning. Resilience is not the absence of stress but the ability to move through it effectively; therefore when they learn strategies to calm their bodies, manage their emotions and reframe their thoughts, they strengthen the neural pathways associated with regulation and recovery (Perry and Szalavitz, 2017). Over time this builds what neuroscientists call stress tolerance, the capacity to remain flexible and composed when faced with challenge.

The development of stress management skills contributes to resilience in several ways. Children who understand their stress responses are less likely to experience emotional overwhelm, allowing for greater emotional stability. Managing stress also supports concentration, memory and problem solving, as high cortisol levels can impair cognitive clarity. Calming techniques such as controlled breathing and movement reduce physiological arousal, helping the body return to calm and promoting physical regulation. When they can manage stress, they communicate more effectively, seek help when needed and build positive social connections. This helps them recognise that they can influence how they feel, building confidence, a sense of agency and self-efficacy, all of which are central to resilience (Bandura, 1997).

Stress and the Brain

When we experience stress the brain releases stress hormones such as cortisol and adrenaline. These chemicals prepare the body to fight, flee or freeze, a survival mechanism known as the stress response. While short bursts of stress can be motivating and even beneficial, prolonged exposure to stress without recovery can have negative effects on health, behaviour and learning, this is known as toxic stress (Shonkoff et al., 2012).

Toxic stress can lead to a range of physical, emotional and cognitive difficulties. Children may experience poor concentration and memory, increased irritability or aggression, disrupted sleep and a reduced immune response. Over time these physiological changes can contribute to feelings of anxiety, helplessness and emotional exhaustion. Understanding this process helps both adults and children see that stress is not a weakness, but a natural biological response designed to keep us safe. The goal is not to eliminate stress altogether but to recognise it early, manage it effectively and develop strategies that help the body and mind recover. The capacity to move through distress and regain steadiness, rather than remain overwhelmed, underpins effective stress management and resilience.

The Resilience Zone

The concept of the Resilience Zone provides a framework for understanding how the autonomic nervous system (ANS) regulates emotional and physiological balance. When individuals are within their resilience zone, their nervous system maintains a flexible rhythm that allows them to manage challenges, recover from stress and return to equilibrium. When this rhythm becomes disrupted, they may experience dysregulation, becoming stuck in a state of high arousal or low arousal. These states can present as various physical, emotional or behavioural symptoms. For example, being stuck on high may lead to anxiety, irritability or hypervigilance, while being stuck on low can result in fatigue, withdrawal or emotional numbness.

Visual tools such as simple graphics showing the resilience zone, can help children understand how their body and emotions respond to stress. This neuroeducation approach explains, in accessible language, what happens in the brain and body when we feel under threat or pressure, helping children make sense of their reactions and feel more confident using self-regulation strategies. As they learn to recognise early signs of imbalance, they are better able to use practical techniques to return to their resilience zone. Over time, this strengthens sensory awareness and supports children to reconnect with bodily cues, building emotional regulation and resilience.

Practical Ways to Teach Emotional Regulation and Stress Management

The following activities last between 20 and 40 minutes and are designed for children aged 7 to 14, with adaptations made as needed for younger or older children. Each activity is structured under the following headings: Purpose, Instructions, Discussion Prompts and Extension or Adaptation. It is important to maintain emotional safety by ensuring that all contributions are respected and valued and by reinforcing that resilience grows through experience and reflection rather than through perfection.

Activity: Safe Place

Purpose

This activity enables children to explore what safety, calm and belonging feel like for them. Understanding their own sources of emotional security strengthens resilience by helping them recognise the conditions that support learning, connection and self-regulation.

Instructions

Begin by creating a quiet, unhurried atmosphere, explaining that everyone needs spaces, people or moments that help them feel settled and accepted and that these safe places can be real or imagined. Invite each to spend 10 to15 minutes drawing or writing about their own 'safe place'. Encourage detailed sensory reflection: "What might they see, hear, smell or feel there?" "What makes this place feel secure or comforting?" Provide reassurance that there is no right or wrong answer. Once the activity is complete, gently offer the option to share their work with a friend, small group or trusted adult. Finish with a short reflection, guiding them to notice how feeling safe supports concentration, confidence and the willingness to try new or challenging tasks. Remind the group that identifying what helps them feel safe can be a useful strategy when they face moments of pressure or uncertainty in their education setting.

Discussion Prompts

Use these prompts to open a reflective conversation about what safety feels like and the small actions that help us create a sense of calm and security.

- What does feeling safe feel like for you?
- What can you see, hear, smell or feel in your 'safe place'?
- How does feeling safe help you when things are hard?
- What little things or routines help you feel safe during the day?

Extension or Adaptation Options

Use visual templates or simple sentence starters for younger children to help them describe or draw their 'safe place' more easily. Older children may explore how to recreate the feelings of their 'safe place' in real life by practising grounding techniques, developing calming routines or thinking about the people who help them feel settled and supported. For those with additional needs, offer options such as collage, sensory materials or verbal storytelling to make the activity more accessible. Encourage families to talk about 'safe place' at home, helping adults understand what supports their child to feel calm, secure and ready to learn.

Activity: Calm Corner

Purpose

The 'calm corner' offers children a supportive space to pause, reset and practise self-regulation; it encourages them to notice early signs of emotional stress, choose appropriate strategies and return to learning with increased focus and confidence. Over time this gentle routine strengthens resilience by normalising emotional awareness and modelling respectful, compassionate responses within the setting.

Instructions

Select a quiet, easily accessible area and establish it clearly as a wellbeing space rather than a consequence-based zone. Aim for a warm, uncluttered feel using soft textures, neutral or calming colours and simple sensory objects. Involve them from the outset, ask what helps them feel grounded and invite contributions such as drawings, affirmation cards or preferred sensory items; this helps build ownership and shared responsibility. Introduce the 'calm corner' to the group with a clear explanation of its purpose to help them notice, regulate and recover, not to separate or exclude. Together create a 'calm menu' displaying three to six simple strategies such as slow breathing, grounding techniques, gentle stretching or brief creative tasks. Remember, keep the language supportive and accessible.

Invite each to develop a personal 'calm card' listing their preferred strategies, store these where they can be accessed independently. Encourage short visits of around five to ten minutes followed by a calm, supported return to activity. Revisit the space often, refreshing resources and celebrating its effective use, finish by modelling the message that choosing to regulate is a strength.

Discussion Prompts

Use these questions to think about how the 'calm corner' helps them take a break, reset and get ready to learn or connect again.

- How can you tell when you need a little break to calm down or feel more in control?
- Which calming ideas work best for you and what makes them helpful?
- How does spending a few minutes in the 'calm corner' help you get ready to learn or play with others?
- What can we all do to look after this space and keep it welcoming for everyone?
- How might these calming skills help you in other places, like at home or when you are out and about?

Extension or Adaptation Options

Use visual emotion cards or puppets with younger children to help them recognise and communicate their feelings more easily. For older children, introduce simple neuroscience to explore what happens in the brain and body during stress and calm states, helping them understand why regulation strategies are effective. In home settings, encourage the creation of a small 'calm space' or a digital calm kit that includes soothing images, sounds or short guided breathing clips. Families can be invited to contribute comforting resources or familiar items to strengthen consistency between home and education environments and support them in using the same strategies across settings.

Activity: The Science of Breathing

Purpose

This activity introduces children to the science and practice of controlled breathing as a foundation for emotional regulation. It helps them notice how their breathing patterns influence their physical state, attention and capacity to respond constructively when under pressure.

Instructions

Begin by explaining that breathing is both automatic and controllable, making it a powerful self-regulation tool. When breaths are slow and steady, the body's calming system signals safety and reduces physiological stress responses; faster shallower breaths can do the opposite, keeping the body alert and tense. Briefly discuss with the group how breathing affects their thoughts, emotions and bodily sensations and invite them to sit comfortably, feet grounded, with eyes gently closed or softly focused. Choose one technique and model it clearly:

- Box Breathing: Inhale for four seconds, hold for four, exhale for four, hold for four.
- Balloon Breathing: One hand on the stomach, imagine a balloon inflating on the in-breath and deflating on the out-breath.
- Smell the Flower and Blow the Candle: Slow breath in through the nose, long breath out through the mouth.
- Counting Breaths: Inhale for three, exhale for five, emphasising the longer out-breath.

Guide the group through two to three minutes of steady practice. Encourage them to notice subtle changes such as heartbeat, warmth, muscle tension, without judging or trying to get it right. Reassure them that each body responds differently and that consistency builds confidence in using these techniques during moments of challenge.

Discussion Prompts

Use these questions to help them think about how their body feels and how calm breathing can help them stay focused, handle big feelings and show kindness to others.

- What did you feel happening in your body before we started and after we finished?
- Which breathing exercise felt the nicest or helped you feel the most calm?
- When do you think these breathing ideas could help you feel more focused or deal with strong feelings?
- How could calm breathing help someone else who is feeling upset or overwhelmed?

Extension or Adaptation Options

With younger children, use bubbles, feathers or pinwheels to make their breath visible and turn the activity into a simple, playful experience. For older children, briefly explain how controlled breathing helps the brain focus or supports the body in calming down after stress. In one-to-one work, guide them to create a personalised calm breathing plan with their preferred techniques. For those with additional needs, provide clear visual cues, short step-by-step instructions or tactile prompts to help them follow the activity confidently.

Activity: Mindful Moment Practice

Purpose

This activity supports children to build self-awareness, calm their nervous system and strengthen emotional regulation. Short regular mindful pauses help them return to the present moment, creating the steady internal conditions that underpin resilience, wellbeing and readiness to engage with learning.

Instructions

Create a calm, predictable space where interruptions are limited and ask them to sit at their desks, on chairs or on the floor, ensuring each has a comfortable personal space. A visual timer can offer reassurance about duration. Invite them to settle into a steady position and either gently close their eyes or lower their gaze. Using a warm, unhurried tone, guide them through the following script, pausing often to allow them to process. For example, "Take a slow breath in through your nose . . . and a long breath out through your mouth . . . Notice your feet on the floor and your hands resting where they naturally fall . . . Feel the weight of your body being supported . . . Thoughts may appear . . . notice them and let them drift past without judgement . . . Bring your attention back to your breath and the sensations of simply sitting and being."

Allow around two to three minutes, when bringing the activity to a close, invite them to open their eyes when ready and take a moment to notice any changes in their body or mood. Emphasise that mindfulness is a gentle practice and that each experience will be different.

Discussion Prompts

Use these questions to help them think about how a mindful moment affects their body, their attention and how they refocus when things feel busy or stressful.

- What did you feel happening in your body during the mindful moment?
- What happened to your attention - did it stay with you or did it wander off?
- What helped you bring your focus back when your mind drifted away?
- When do you think taking a short mindful pause could help you during a busy or tricky moment?

Extension or Adaptation Options

Younger children may benefit from simple breathing images; older children might prefer mindful listening, slow walking or gentle stretching to help them stay engaged. For those who find stillness difficult or overstimulating, offer grounding objects to hold, to keep their eyes open, or light movement so they can participate comfortably. In one-to-one or alternative provision settings, adjust the length of the activity, the position they sit or stand in, and how much guidance you provide to match their individual needs.

Activity: See It, Own It, Change It

Purpose

This activity helps children recognise their body's early stress signals, understand what these signals mean and practise simple strategies to restore calm. It supports emotional literacy, personal responsibility and the development of resilient habits that can be applied across the education setting and home.

Instructions

Begin by explaining that everyone has an internal alarm system designed to protect them. Sometimes this alarm switches on during everyday challenges before a test, after a tense interaction or when walking into a busy room. These moments can trigger changes such as a racing heart, tight shoulders, shaky hands or an uncomfortable feeling in the stomach.

Emphasise that resilience grows when those signals are noticed early and responded to with purposeful, calming action. Share two or three short examples to make the idea concrete, such as "You are about to speak in front of others and your chest feels tight", or "A friend walks past without speaking and your stomach drops." Invite them to choose one example from their own life to work through, then guide them through these three steps:

- See It: Ask them to describe the physical signals that tell them their internal alarm is active.
- Own It: Support them to explore how they usually respond. "Does your reaction help the situation or add pressure?" "What alternatives might be available?"
- Change It: Introduce a range of regulation strategies and demonstrate a few, such as slow breathing, grounding techniques, stretching, gentle movement or a sensory tool. Encourage them to select at least one they can realistically use next time.

Discussion Prompts

Use these prompts to help them explore how their bodies react to stress and how early awareness can support calmer choices in difficult moments.

- How does your body let you know you're starting to feel stressed or upset?
- What happens to your thoughts or actions when your body starts to feel calm again?
- Why is it helpful to notice the very first tiny sign that you're getting stressed?
- How could noticing these signs help you when things get tricky?

Extension or Adaptation Options

For younger children simplify the activity to two clear steps: first notice it and then do it. Use visual prompts, simple pictures or body outlines to help them identify where they feel stress in their bodies and what they can do to calm down. Extend the activity by introducing journalling, personal regulation plans or role-play scenarios so they can practise responding to tricky moments. In one-to-one sessions or alternative provision settings, build in sensory resources such as fiddle toys, textured objects or grounding tools to help them connect with their bodies and regulate more effectively. Families can also be invited to learn and use a shared calming strategy at home.

Activity: Zones of Comfort, Stretch and Panic

Purpose

This activity supports children to recognise how they respond to challenge, pressure and uncertainty. By exploring three familiar zones, 'comfort', 'stretch' and 'panic', they build self-awareness and begin to understand how emotional regulation supports resilience. The aim is to help them notice when they are edging towards overwhelm and to practise strategies that bring them back to a manageable learning-ready state.

Instructions

Prepare three concentric circles on a large sheet or whiteboard. Label the centre circle in green 'comfort', the middle in yellow 'stretch' and the outside in red 'panic'. Begin by explaining that everyone moves between these zones throughout the day and that the 'stretch' zone is where growth happens. Offer simple examples for each: 'comfort' might be a familiar hobby, 'stretch' could be attempting something new, 'panic' feels unsafe or too much.

Invite them to share everyday examples of when they have been in each zone. Add these around the circles, keeping the focus on non-sensitive scenarios such as joining an activity, tackling a tricky task or meeting new people. Shift the discussion to bodily and thinking cues. For example, ask "What does your body do in each zone?" and "What do your thoughts sound like?" Explore signs such as steady breathing in 'comfort' or tense shoulders in 'panic'.

Introduce a small toolkit of regulation strategies and demonstrate calm breathing, grounding through the senses and reassuring self-talk. Discuss which strategies might be useful in each zone and why. Give each a sticky note to write one strategy they will use when they notice themselves moving towards 'panic'; place these in the 'stretch' zone as shared reminders. Finish by reinforcing that resilience grows when they recognise their limits early and use strategies to stay grounded and engaged.

Discussion Prompts

Use these prompts to help them recognise their learning zones, understand why new experiences can feel uncomfortable and explore strategies for staying in a healthy 'stretch' zone.

- How can you tell when you're in your 'stretch' zone, the place where you're learning something new but still feel safe enough to try?
- Why do new things sometimes feel a bit strange or uncomfortable at the start?
- What clues does your body or mind give you when you're getting too overwhelmed and starting to move towards the 'panic' zone?
- What could you do to help yourself get back to your 'stretch' zone or your 'comfort' zone?

Extension or Adaptation Options

For younger children, use coloured hoops, floor spots or simple movement-based games to help them experience the different zones with their bodies. For example, they can step into the 'comfort', 'stretch' or 'panic' hoops to show how each zone feels. For older children, extend the activity into real-life discussions about situations such as exams, teamwork, friendships or education transitions, helping them recognise which zone they are likely to be in and what might help them stay in the 'stretch' zone. In one-to-one or SEND/ALN settings, simplify the language, use visual supports such as symbols, pictures or colour-coded cards, and focus on one regulation tool at a time so they can practise and feel confident before adding anything new.

Activity: What I Can and Can't Control

Purpose

This activity supports children to distinguish between what sits within their control and what does not. By making this distinction explicit, they learn to redirect their attention towards manageable actions, reducing feelings of overwhelm and strengthening everyday resilience.

Instructions

Introduce the idea that all of us, regardless of age, sometimes feel unsettled when life presents situations we cannot influence. Explain that the circle of control is a simple, practical way to help us notice what we can influence and where it is most helpful to focus our energy. Provide each with paper and colouring materials and, on a board or screen, draw two circles, a small circle inside a larger one. Label the inner circle 'things I can control' and the outer circle 'things I can't control'. In the inner circle, include items such as my effort, my words, how I treat others and how I respond when plans change. In the outer circle, offer examples such as other people's reactions, the weather, unexpected events or traffic.

Invite them to create their own circles and encourage them to use words, drawings or symbols to express their ideas. As they work, gently check understanding by asking questions such as, "Is this something you can change or can you only choose how you react to it?" Once complete, ask them to review their circles and notice patterns. Finish with a brief guided reflection, emphasising that confidence often grows when we focus on what we can influence.

Discussion Prompts

Use these prompts to help them explore the difference between focusing on what they can control and letting go of what they cannot and how this shift can reduce overwhelm.

- How do you feel when you think about the things you can control or change?
- What happens when you keep worrying about things you can't change no matter what you do?
- Can you think of a time when you stopped worrying about something you couldn't control and it helped you feel better?
- What could you try next time something feels too big or overwhelming?

Extension or Adaptation Options

For younger children, provide pre-drawn circles, pictures or simple examples to help them sort 'what I can control' and 'what I can't control'. Older children can extend the task by writing a short reflection, creating a personal action plan or thinking about how they want to respond to similar challenges in the future. This activity also works well as a shared display in a classroom or as a conversation tool during one-to-one discussions with families, helping everyone use the same language and strategies to reduce overwhelm.

Activity: The 4-Factor Approach

Purpose

This activity introduces a simple, structured method to help children understand and navigate strong emotions. By separating facts from assumptions, recognising responsibility, exploring alternative viewpoints and allowing space to pause, they strengthen emotional literacy, flexible thinking and self-regulation, all essential components of resilience in education settings.

Instructions

Prepare a whiteboard, flipchart or scenario cards, for example, 'a friend walks past without speaking', 'someone laughs and you're not sure if it's about you'. Begin by explaining that strong emotions are normal and often helpful, yet when they build quickly, they can cloud clear thinking. The 4-Factor Approach offers a step-by-step process to slow the moment down. Introduce each of the following steps:

- Say what happened: talk about what you saw or heard, without guessing why it happened.
- Know what's yours to manage: think about what you can control and what is not your job to fix.
- Think of another possibility: ask yourself if there could be another reason or way to look at it.
- Take a pause: give yourself a moment to breathe and let strong feelings settle before you respond.

Model the approach using a relatable scenario, thinking aloud so children can hear each step of the reasoning process. For example, "You say hello to someone you know, but they don't reply." Talk through the four steps slowly, making your thinking visible. Next, organise them into small groups and give each group a scenario card. Ask the children to work together to apply the four steps and record their ideas. Bring the group back together to share reflections, focusing on how each step helped slow their thinking and change how the situation felt. Finish with a short individual reflection, such as, "When I feel strong emotions, what helps me pause and think?"

Discussion Prompts

Use these prompts to help them reflect on their own responses, explore the power of pausing and consider how taking appropriate responsibility can shape more positive outcomes in challenging situations.

- Which part of this feels easiest for you and which part feels a bit harder?
- How could taking a pause, even a tiny one, change what happens in a tricky situation?
- What happens when we try to fix or take responsibility for things that aren't actually ours to sort out?
- How could looking at a problem in a different way help you at your setting, at home, or with friends?

Extension or Adaptation Options

For younger children, use role-play, puppets or illustrated prompts to help them act out pausing, taking responsibility or looking at a situation in a new way. Older children can deepen the activity by exploring how their thoughts, emotions and behaviours connect and how a pause or reframe can influence each part of that cycle. For children with additional needs, include visual supports, clear sentence starters and extra processing time so they can work through each idea at their own pace and with confidence. Families can be involved by sending home a simplified version of the activity, helping everyone use the same shared language around emotional regulation and positive responses.

Activity: Refuel for Results

Purpose

To help children recognise that rest, recovery and reflection are vital elements of resilience. They learn that setbacks offer insight and that taking care of themselves is an active strength that supports emotional stamina and sustained effort.

Instructions

Prepare the space by displaying the following quotes where everyone can see them:

- *"If you get tired, learn to rest, not to quit."* Banksy
- *"I've failed over and over and over again in my life and that is why I succeed."* Michael Jordan
- *"Failure is the opportunity to begin again more intelligently."* Henry Ford
- *"Success is not final, failure is not fatal: it is the courage to continue that counts."* Winston Churchill
- *"The only real mistake is the one from which we learn nothing."* Henry Ford

Begin with a short discussion about how people learn, grow and succeed over time. Use examples such as athletes, artists or performers to explore how effort, mistakes, rest and reflection all play a part in progress. Emphasise that setbacks and failures are not signs of weakness, but important opportunities for learning, adjustment and growth.

Support children to make links between physical rest, emotional recovery and the ability to think clearly after a setback or mistake. Discuss how pausing, resting and reflecting can help them return with greater focus, confidence and problem-solving skills. Invite children to choose one quote that stands out to them. In pairs or small groups, ask them to talk about why they chose it and how it connects to their own experiences of trying hard, making mistakes, feeling tired, or facing challenges. Bring the group back together to explore what the quotes collectively teach us about resilience. Highlight that resilience includes continuing after difficulty, learning from mistakes, and knowing when to rest and refuel rather than give up.

Next, support the group to create a shared 'refuel for results' display. Each child adds a personal refuelling or learning strategy, such as taking a break, trying a different approach, asking for help, using movement or creative activities, or adding a meaningful quote. This creates a visual reminder that resilience is built through both effort and recovery. Finish with a brief reflection, asking children how they recognise when they need rest or a change in approach, and which strategies help them recover, learn and keep going.

Discussion Prompts

Use these prompts to help them explore the importance of rest, how taking a break supports their thinking and emotions, and how recharging can prepare them for future challenges.

- Can you think of a time when you just needed a rest in order not to give up completely?
- How does taking a break change the way you think or feel?
- What's the difference between stopping because you've given up and stopping to recharge your energy?
- Which quote do you like the most and what does it mean to you?
- How could resting help you deal with challenges better in the future?

Extension or Adaptation Options

For younger children, use visual symbols such as battery icons, traffic lights or simple pictures to help them explore their energy levels and understand when they need to rest and recharge. With older children, invite them to do a short piece of reflective journalling about a time they moved forwards from a setback, focusing on how rest or recovery helped them. Families can be involved by contributing motivational quotes or positive messages for a class display, helping to reinforce the idea of healthy rest at home as well as in their setting. This activity also links well with learning in PSHE, Physical Education, and English, making it a useful cross-curricular tool for exploring wellbeing, resilience and reflective writing.

Connecting the Learning

As children develop greater awareness of their emotions and learn to recognise the body's early stress signals, they begin to build the internal steadiness that underpins resilience. The strategies explored in this unit support them to pause, regulate and re-engage their thinking when pressure rises. Over time this strengthens emotional literacy, physiological regulation and a growing sense of agency. Emotional regulation and stress management are not about avoiding challenge but about remaining sufficiently calm, connected and flexible to learn from it. When children understand what is happening inside them and have practical tools to restore balance, they are better equipped to navigate relationships, learning demands and unexpected change.

For these skills to embed, they must be within an environment of consistency, safety and connection. Adults play a critical role by modelling calm responses, maintaining predictable routines and responding with empathy rather than urgency. Such environments buffer stress and help children return to their resilience zone more quickly, reinforcing the message that difficult feelings are manageable and support is available. As highlighted throughout this unit, resilience is built through repeated experience of being guided through challenge, not left to cope alone.

This understanding creates a natural bridge to the next unit. While emotional regulation supports children in the moment, long-term wellbeing depends on the everyday habits and routines that sustain balance over time. Unit 6 therefore shifts the focus from responding to stress to proactively maintaining emotional health through self-care. By linking regulation skills with consistent, nurturing self-care practices, children learn not only how to recover from difficulty but how to create the conditions that help them stay well, engaged and ready to learn.

Unit 6
Self-Care as a Protective Factor

What this unit covers:

- Understand how everyday self-care builds resilience through emotional regulation, self-awareness and coping skills.
- Use simple frameworks to identify strengths, supports and strategies, including 'I Have, I Am, I Can' and the 'Five Ways to Wellbeing'.
- Complete practical reflection and creative tasks such as mindful nature walks, resilience-in-nature activities, strength shields, self-care trees and personal self-care toolboxes.

Introduction

Self-care is a concept often associated with adulthood, yet for children it forms a central part of learning how to understand themselves, manage pressure and recover from everyday challenges. In educational settings developing effective self-care habits becomes an essential foundation for resilience. This unit explores self-care not as an extra or occasional activity but as a consistent practice that nurtures emotional balance, strengthens coping skills and supports overall wellbeing.

Drawing on research across psychology, education and child development this unit emphasises that resilience does not emerge suddenly nor rely on exceptional qualities. It develops gradually through repeated experiences in which children learn to recognise their feelings, make small but intentional choices and use strategies that help them regain control when emotions feel overwhelming. To support this learning the unit introduces practical frameworks such as Grotberg's (1997) 'I Have, I Am, I Can' resilience model and the New Economics Foundation's (2008) 'Five Ways to Wellbeing'. These approaches provide clear, accessible language that helps children identify their internal resources, the relationships that support them and the strategies that strengthen their coping. By understanding what keeps them steady, what lifts their mood and what helps them persevere, they are increasingly empowered to take ownership of their emotional health.

DOI: 10.4324/9781003409632-7

Importance of Self-Care

Self-care is a critical component of emotional literacy, resilience and wellbeing for children. While it is often discussed in the context of adults, research increasingly recognises the importance of developing self-care skills early in life. The World Health Organization (2020) defines self-care as "the ability of individuals, families and communities to promote health, prevent disease, maintain health and cope with illness and disability with or without the support of a health-care provider".

Within education, self-care extends beyond physical health to include emotional balance, stress management and self-awareness. Self-awareness is a core component of resilience. It involves understanding one's own thoughts, emotions, strengths and behaviours and recognising how these influence responses to challenges. When children develop self-awareness, they become better able to identify what helps them cope, what triggers stress and how to use their strengths effectively. By learning to notice and name their internal resources, they build a stronger sense of control and confidence, which provides essential foundations for resilience.

Psychological research supports the view that self-care underpins the development of self-efficacy (Bandura, 1997) and growth mindset (Dweck, 2006). When children experience that their actions, such as taking a short break, asking for help or practising relaxation make a difference to how they feel and perform, they strengthen their belief in their own agency. Adults play a vital role in modelling this through everyday practice, demonstrating how small, proactive choices can sustain wellbeing and improve focus, relationships and behaviour.

Self-Care Builds Resilience

Resilience grows through the interaction between internal strengths and external supports (Masten, 2014). Self-care provides the internal structure through which these supports can operate effectively. By learning to notice and meet their own needs, children develop emotional regulation, optimism and perseverance, core components of resilience.

Practising self-care also reinforces adaptive coping mechanisms. According to the American Psychological Association (2014) strategies such as maintaining social connection, engaging in physical activity and practising mindfulness help buffer against stress and promote recovery after adversity. These approaches allow them to respond to challenges rather than react impulsively, making self-care both a preventative and restorative process.

When adults actively promote self-care, they help them to internalise protective habits that strengthen both wellbeing and learning. Over time this fosters a positive feedback loop - improved emotional regulation supports academic focus and social relationships, which in turn increase self-worth and resilience.

Practical Ways to Teach Self-Care

The following activities last between 20 and 40 minutes and are designed for children aged 7 to 14, with adaptations made as needed for younger or older children. Each activity is structured under the following headings: Purpose, Instructions, Discussion Prompts, and Extension or Adaptation. It is important to maintain emotional safety by ensuring that all contributions are respected and valued and by reinforcing that resilience grows through experience and reflection rather than through perfection.

Activity: Walking in Nature

Purpose

This activity introduces children to the restorative impact of spending time outdoors. Through gentle, mindful attention to the natural world they learn to recognise how external environments shape internal states, supporting emotional regulation, grounding and everyday resilience.

Instructions

Identify a safe, accessible outdoor space such as the education setting grounds, a courtyard or a nearby park. Complete any required checks and ensure the route is manageable for all. Begin by explaining that the group will take a slow, mindful walk designed to help them notice what is happening around and within them. Invite the group to start by standing still and taking one steady breath. Encourage them to walk quietly, noticing what they can see, for example shapes, colours, movement: what they hear, for example, birds, wind, distant sounds; what they feel, for example, air, textures, footsteps: and what they can smell, for example, earth, plants, fresh air. Keep the pace unhurried and periodically pause to deepen awareness. A short silent moment can help them tune into subtle details.

As they walk, offer light prompts such as, "What is the smallest sound you can hear?" or "Notice how your body feels right now." When back indoors provide time for drawing or writing about what they observed and how their emotions or focus shifted before, during and after the walk. Finish with a brief review emphasising how regular contact with nature can restore calm and clarity.

Discussion Prompts

Use these questions to explore how spending a mindful moment in nature affected their thoughts feelings and awareness.

- Did your mood or energy change at all? How did you feel before the walk and how did you feel afterwards?
- What things did you see, hear or feel that really caught your attention?
- Did anything outside surprise you or make you think, "Oh! That's different!"?
- When do you think taking a calm, quiet moment outside might help you feel more settled?
- Which small things were easy to notice and which ones were a bit harder to spot?

Extension or Adaptation Options

Create a 'calm collection' using natural items such as leaves, stones or feathers to represent comfort and grounding. Children can explore what each item means to them and how it might help them feel steady. For a longer activity, begin a multi-day nature reflection journal, where the record what they notice outdoors and how it affects their mood or focus. Use tactile objects or visual supports for those with sensory sensitivities to help them engage in a way that feels safe and comfortable. If going outside is not possible, recreate the experience indoors using plants, natural materials, photographs or recorded outdoor sounds to provide a similar calming atmosphere.

Activity: Resilience in Nature

Purpose

This activity supports children to understand resilience by observing how the natural world adapts, endures and restores itself. Through careful noticing and guided reflection, they begin to recognise parallels between nature's responses to challenge and their own capacity to recover, regulate and grow.

Instructions

Begin by introducing resilience as something we can observe in nature, offering a few clear examples such as a tree bending with the wind, new shoots appearing after a hard winter or a weed growing strongly in an unexpected place. Invite children to explore their surroundings, look closely at provided images or think about outdoor places they know well. Ask them to choose one natural example that in their view, shows determination or renewal. Encourage them to describe exactly what makes their chosen example resilient, for instance, its flexibility, patience, persistence or ability to repair and keep growing.

Bring the group together and read or play 'The Rose That Grew from Concrete' by Tupac Shakur (1999). Prompt them to think about what the concrete might represent in real life: pressure, barriers, expectations or change. Provide time and space for creative expression, offer options such as drawing, writing, collage or simple photography. Emphasise that there is no right way; the aim is to express a personal understanding of resilience. Finish by inviting those who wish to share their work. Support the group to create a collective display, illustrating the many ways resilience appears across nature and within ourselves.

Discussion Prompts

Use these questions to explore how ideas from nature can help them understand their own resilience and what supports them during tough times.

- Which example from nature feels most like you and what makes you think that?
- If you had some concrete in your life right now, what might it stand for, something tricky, something in the way or something that feels heavy?
- When things feel tough what helps you keep going or feel a little better inside?
- How can being strong on the inside sometimes be quiet or hard for other people to notice like the way some plants grow even in tiny spaces?

Extension or Adaptation Options

Use outdoor exploration with younger children, encouraging them to notice real-life examples of resilience in nature such as plants, weather patterns or wildlife. Older children can extend the activity through reflective writing, poetry or digital storytelling, using photos or short videos to express what resilience means to them. For sensory-based or one-to-one work, provide tactile materials such as leaves, fabric, sandpaper or natural textures to help them create a textured collage that represents strength and growth. Invite families to contribute their own examples of resilience in nature for a shared display, helping children see how these ideas connect across their different environments.

Activity: My Strength Shield

Purpose

This activity supports children to recognise the strengths that help them manage challenges and adapt to change. Drawing on the 'I Have, I Am, I Can' resilience framework (Grotberg, 1997), it invites them to identify the personal qualities, skills, relationships and achievements that form their internal and external support system. By shifting attention from what is difficult to what is strong, the activity nurtures confidence, self-awareness and a belief that resilience can grow with practice.

Instructions

Begin by explaining that strengths are the positive qualities, skills and supports that enable us to cope, learn and keep going during tougher moments. Reinforce that everyone has strengths, even if some are less visible or harder to name. Show the 'strength shield' template divided into three sections. Walk through each section, linking it clearly to the resilience framework:

- I Am (Personal Qualities): for example, being patient, hopeful, calm, curious, determined or caring.
- I Can (Skills and Capabilities): such as solving problems, asking for help, trying again, taking a break when needed or supporting others.
- I Have (People and Supports): including trusted adults, friends, clubs, pets, routines, or safe spaces that help them feel grounded.

Provide creative materials or digital templates and invite them to fill their shield using words, drawings, colours or symbols. Encourage the children to choose the method that feels most comfortable. Once complete, invite them to share one section with a friend or small group, focusing on what they discovered about themselves and how these strengths show up in daily life.

Discussion Prompts

Use these questions to help you think about your strengths and how they support you when things feel tricky.

- Which of your strengths do you use the most when something feels difficult?
- Who or what helps you use your strengths when you need them?
- Can you remember a time when one of your strengths helped you handle a tough moment?
- Which of your strengths could help you with something you are working on right now?

Extension or Adaptation Options

For younger children or those with communication needs, offer symbol-supported templates or strength cards so they can choose pictures or words that represent their abilities. For older children, take the activity further by linking their identified strengths to a personal goal they are working towards. They may also choose one 'I Can' strength to focus on and deliberately practise over the next month, helping them build confidence and see how strengths grow with use. In group settings, create a shared wall of strength where everyone can contribute an example, helping the group recognise the wide range of strengths within their community.

Activity: I Am Resilient

Purpose

This activity helps children identify what steadies them when life feels challenging. By naming the people, places and practices that support their wellbeing, they begin to recognise the internal and external resources that strengthen their resilience. The shared display reinforces a sense of connection and collective capability.

Instructions

Prepare a display titled 'my sources of strength' and explain that everyone has strategies they rely on when they feel overwhelmed, worried or unsure and the task is to notice what genuinely helps. Provide each with a stone and invite them to personalise it using words, drawings or symbols that represent what helps them feel grounded, calm or capable.

Encourage thoughtful reflection by offering gentle, open prompts such as "Who supports you when things are difficult?", "Where do you feel most settled?" or "What helps you keep going when something feels tough?" Allow quiet time for thinking. When finished, ask them to place their stones on the display, emphasising that every contribution matters and that resilience can look very different from one person to another. Finish with a short whole-group reflection using the prompts below to deepen understanding and highlight the value of noticing strengths both familiar and newly discovered.

Discussion Prompts

Use these questions to help them think about all the strengths in the group and what they might mean for them.

- What do you notice about all the different strengths and ideas on our display?
- Is there something on someone else's stone that you might want to try or learn more about?
- How do you know when it is the right time to use one of your strategies to help you calm down or cope?
- How does it feel to see everyone's strengths together in one place?
- What new strength or strategy might you want to add in the future as you get even better at being resilient?

Extension or Adaptation Options

Offer pre-drawn symbols for younger children, helping them choose pictures that represent their strengths without needing to write or draw independently. Older children can take the activity further by reflecting on how their strengths show up in different places, at home, in the setting or with friends, and noticing which strengths stay the same and which ones change. In one-to-one or small-group work, add a new stone each session to create a personalised strength pathway, showing how their confidence grows over time. Families can also be invited to contribute their own stones or ideas, helping to strengthen the connection between home and the education setting and reinforcing shared language around resilience.

Activity: The Self-Care Tree

Purpose

This activity helps children recognise how everyday habits, choices and supportive relationships contribute to their resilience. By using the metaphor of a tree, they can visualise how strong foundations, steady routines and uplifting experiences work together to sustain wellbeing, especially during times of pressure or change.

Instructions

Provide each with paper or display a large outline of a tree and explain that the tree represents how we care for ourselves over time, not just when things feel difficult. Emphasise that resilience is built through small, consistent actions that help us recover, reset and keep going. Begin with the roots and invite them to write or draw the essentials that help them feel safe and settled. These may include sleep, predictable routines, supportive adults or access to calming spaces; encourage brief discussion about why these foundations matter.

Move to the trunk and ask them to identify strengths, personal qualities and daily habits that help keep them steady. Examples might include compassion, humour, practising gratitude, physical activity or asking for help when needed. Finally explore the branches and leaves; they can add the activities, relationships and interests that bring joy, connection and energy. These could include creative activities, time outdoors, friendships or moments of stillness. Once completed, invite them to share one element that strengthens them. Reassure the group that every tree will look different because self-care is personal and influenced by experience, culture and context. Display the trees together as a collective reminder of shared commitment to wellbeing.

Discussion Prompts

Use these questions to help them think about their resilience tree and how the different parts of it support them in everyday life.

- Which parts of your tree feel the strongest right now?
- Are there any parts you might want to give a little more care, time or support?
- Who helps you look after yourself and what do they do that helps?
- When life feels a bit tough, which parts of your tree help you stay calm or steady?

Extension or Adaptation Options

Younger children may benefit from using symbols, images or tactile materials such as textured leaves, felt or string to help them build their tree in a hands-on, engaging way. Older children can extend the activity by linking different parts of their tree to specific pressures they are managing, such as exams, friendships or changes at home, helping them see how their self-care habits support them in real-life situations. Families can also create trees together at home, using the activity to explore shared needs, personal strengths and the different ways each family member looks after their wellbeing.

Activity: My Self-Care Toolbox

Purpose

This activity supports children to identify, practise and value the strategies that help them stay steady during emotionally demanding moments. By creating a personalised 'self-care toolbox', they build awareness of what regulates them, why it works and how to use it early before emotions feel unmanageable. This strengthens agency and nurtures resilient habits they can draw on across settings.

Instructions

Provide each child with a small box, envelope or folded card labelled 'my self-care toolbox', plus pens, scissors and small slips of paper. Begin by explaining that self-care is not a luxury; it is a practical way of supporting our emotional health, particularly when life feels tough.

Emphasise that everyone's needs are different and effective tools are those that genuinely help them feel calmer, safer or more grounded. Invite them to think of five personal tools they use or could try and offer prompts across several categories:

- Calming actions, for example, walking, drawing, music, breathing techniques.
- Supportive people, such as a trusted adult, friend or family member.
- Helpful thoughts, for example, "I can get through this" or "This feeling will ease."
- Comforting spaces or items such as a quiet corner, a pet or a familiar object.

Ask them to write or draw one idea per slip and place these in their toolbox and encourage decoration to make the toolbox meaningful and easy to recognise. When ready, invite them to share one tool, reinforcing that every toolbox will be different and that this diversity is positive.

Discussion Prompts

Use these questions to help them think about their emotional toolbox and how it can support them when their feelings start to feel big or overwhelming.

- Which tools do you think you could really use when your feelings start to grow?
- What might make some tools harder to remember and what could help you remember them more easily?
- Who helps you notice the moments when you might need to use one of your tools?
- How does having your toolbox ready before you need it change how you feel about tricky or worrying situations in the future?

Extension or Adaptation Options

Younger children may prefer using symbols, stickers or simple drawings to represent their tools, while older children might enjoy creating a digital version of their toolbox using photos, apps or short videos. Revisit toolboxes in one-to-one sessions to review which strategies are working well and to add new ideas as they grow in confidence and self-awareness. In group settings create a shared strengths or strategies display using anonymous contributions from each person, helping children see the wide range of tools others find helpful. Families can also be invited to make their own toolboxes at home, helping everyone develop a shared language around wellbeing and strengthening the connection between home and the education setting.

Connecting the Learning

As children engage in self-care in consistent and purposeful ways, they begin to develop the inner steadiness that allows them to notice their feelings, regulate their responses and recover more quickly from everyday pressures. These habits do not emerge by chance; they are taught, practised and reinforced over time, forming a vital foundation for resilience through increased self-awareness, emotional regulation and a growing sense of personal agency. When children recognise that small, manageable actions can positively influence how they feel and cope, they start to trust their own ability to manage challenge.

This learning is firmly grounded in evidence. Research on self-efficacy (Bandura, 1997) and growth mindset (Dweck, 2006) highlights the importance of children experiencing themselves as capable of influencing outcomes, while resilience frameworks such as Grotberg's (1997) 'I Have, I Am, I Can' model emphasise the interplay between internal strengths and external supports. When self-care is embedded through predictable routines, positive relationships, access to calming spaces and everyday practices aligned with the 'Five Ways to Wellbeing' (New Economics Foundation, 2008), children learn that wellbeing is sustained through ordinary, repeatable choices rather than exceptional effort.

Importantly, self-care is not separate from learning, it enables it. When adults model self-care openly and integrate it into daily practice, they send a clear message that noticing emotions, asking for support and taking restorative pauses are signs of strength. Over time, this normalises emotional awareness and adaptive coping within the learning environment, creating conditions in which children feel safe to acknowledge difficulty and confident in their capacity to respond.

This unit therefore marks a point of consolidation rather than completion. While self-care strengthens emotional balance and coping, resilience is also shaped by how children interpret and make sense of challenge. The next phase of learning moves beyond regulation towards meaning. Unit 7 builds directly on this foundation by exploring how optimism, curiosity and realistic hope can be intentionally developed, supporting children to view setbacks with perspective, recognise progress and sustain confidence in their ability to grow.

Unit 7

Developing a Positive and Realistic Mindset

What this unit covers:

- Build a positive, realistic mindset to strengthen resilience, hope and confidence when facing setbacks.
- Develop skills in belonging, kindness, gratitude and growth mindset to support optimism, perseverance and emotional regulation.
- Complete practical activities such as belonging maps, kindness challenges, I Wonder . . . prompts and Three Good Things reflections.

Introduction

Building resilience begins with how children view themselves and their challenges. A positive and realistic outlook is not about pretending things are fine, it is about helping them notice what is going well, hold onto hope and believe that difficulties can be worked through with the right support (Snyder, 2002; Fredrickson, 2001). In education settings this mindset is shaped every day through the messages they receive about their strengths, progress and value within the community. For some optimism does not come easily and experiences of uncertainty, stress or disrupted relationships can make looking ahead feel unsafe. This is why developing a positive outlook relies on more than positive language alone. It requires predictable routines, emotionally available adults and environments where effort, honesty and belonging are consistently reinforced (Shonkoff, 2016; Siegel and Bryson, 2011).

This unit explores how positivity and realism work together to strengthen resilience. Drawing on psychological research and focusing on simple, age-appropriate practices such as gratitude (Emmons and McCullough, 2003), noticing success and valuing small acts of kindness help train the mind to see possibility as well as difficulty. Models like Seligman's PERMA framework show that wellbeing grows from positive emotions, engagement, relationships, meaning and achievement, all of which can be intentionally nurtured in daily education setting life (Norrish et al., 2013). A positive and realistic outlook prepares them

DOI: 10.4324/9781003409632-8

for the next step in resilience development, learning to manage stress and cope constructively when emotions rise. This unit sets the foundation for those skills by showing that hope and challenge can sit side by side and that with guidance, they can navigate both with increasing confidence.

Importance of a Positive and Realistic Mindset

Developing a positive outlook in children is not about ignoring challenges or pretending that everything is fine. It is about encouraging a mindset that allows them to notice what is going well, to respond with optimism rather than defeat and to build resilience when faced with setbacks. Research consistently shows that a positive outlook is closely linked to increased motivation, improved relationships and better mental health outcomes (Seligman, 2011; Keyes, 2019). However, it is important to recognise that not all children find optimism easy.

Research into Adverse Childhood Experiences (ACEs) such as exposure to abuse, neglect, or household dysfunction shows that when they experience four or more ACEs they are significantly less likely to display optimism or a hopeful outlook about their future (Felitti et al., 1998; Bellis et al., 2014). These early experiences can shape the developing brain, influencing how children perceive safety, trust and possibility. Developing a positive outlook requires consistent support, relational safety and opportunities to experience success and belonging. In education this means helping them to see themselves as capable, to recognise their own progress and to view mistakes as part of the learning process rather than evidence of failure. When education settings create a culture that actively promotes optimism, gratitude and belonging they are not only happier but also more engaged and successful (Riley, 2019; Wang and Eccles, 2012).

A Positive Mindset Builds Resilience

A positive and realistic outlook acts as a protective factor in the development of resilience. It supports a child's capacity to recover from setbacks, manage uncertainty and sustain hope in challenging circumstances. Resilience researchers such as Masten describe this as ordinary magic, the ability to adapt successfully despite adversity (Masten, 2014). Optimism does not remove difficulty but instead it shapes how they interpret it.

Bandura's theory of self-efficacy explains that individuals who believe in their ability to influence outcomes are more likely to persist through challenge (Bandura, 1997). Dweck's work on growth mindset shows that children who interpret effort and setbacks as opportunities for growth are more likely to develop emotional endurance (Dweck, 2006).These perspectives are central to resilience; when they hold a balanced belief that things can improve through effort, connection and support, they are better equipped to regulate emotion and recover from disappointment.

Adults can nurture this outlook by combining cognitive and emotional approaches. Teaching them to identify helpful and unhelpful thoughts, to name and normalise emotions and to notice small daily successes strengthens their internal resilience systems. Over time this supports both self-regulation and perseverance, which are two key components of learning under pressure.

Practical Ways to Teach a Positive and Realistic Outlook

The following activities last between 20 and 40 minutes and are designed for children aged 7 to 14, with adaptations made as needed for younger or older children. Each activity is structured under the following headings, Purpose, Instructions, Discussion Prompts, and Extension or Adaptation. It is important to maintain emotional safety by ensuring that all contributions are respected and valued and by reinforcing that resilience grows through experience and reflection rather than through perfection.

Activity: Belonging Web

Purpose

This activity supports children to recognise the connections that link them to others. By making these links visible they experience a stronger sense of acceptance, emotional safety and shared responsibility key ingredients for building resilience in education settings.

Instructions

Begin by explaining that everyone has a fundamental need to feel that they belong, and that this sense of belonging is built through everyday connections, both big and small. Next, draw a large circle or simple web shape on the board or floor and write Our Community at the centre. Give each child a card or sticky note and ask them to write their name clearly. Invite them to place their name around the circle. Once all names are in position, guide the group to look for something they share with at least one other person in the room. This could be a shared interest, experience, value or preference. For example, they might like the same type of music, enjoy outdoor activities, speak another language, care for animals or value kindness.

As they identify a shared connection, ask them to attach a piece of string or tape between the two names. Continue until a visible web forms. If some struggle to identify a link, gently support them by suggesting possible shared experiences or inviting peers to offer inclusive connections. Pause occasionally to highlight how the web expands and strengthens as more links are added, emphasising that everyone contributes to the community's overall sense of safety and inclusion.

Discussion Prompts

Use the following prompts to guide a reflective discussion on belonging, connection and the small everyday actions that help everyone feel included.

- What helps you feel like you belong in this group?
- How does feeling connected to others make it easier to learn or try new things?
- What small things can we do each day to help others feel included and cared for?
- How can you tell if someone feels left out and what could you do to help them feel part of the group?

Extension or Adaptation Options

Use pictures or coloured threads for younger children to make their connections more concrete and easier to understand. Older children can develop a personal Belonging Map, helping them identify the people, places and activities that make them feel supported and grounded. In one-to-one or small-group sessions, create a focused mini-web that explores relationships with trusted peers or adults, allowing for deeper conversation. Families can also be encouraged to create a home belonging web, helping them recognise support in different parts of their lives and strengthening the link between education setting and family.

Activity: Coat of Arms of Belonging

Purpose

This activity supports children to recognise the relationships, places and values that help them feel connected and safe. By exploring belonging in this structured yet creative way, they build a clearer sense of identity and community, key protective factors in resilience.

Instructions

Begin by introducing belonging as the feeling of being accepted, valued and connected to others. Explain that they often belong to multiple groups and that these connections can strengthen confidence and wellbeing. Provide each child with a blank shield template or plain paper. Ask them to divide their shield into four sections and guide them to fill each section with drawings, key words or simple symbols representing:

- People who support and care for them.
- Groups, communities or places where they feel a sense of connection.
- Personal values or qualities they want to uphold.
- Things that help them feel safe, calm or grounded.

Allow quiet time for thoughtful creativity, reassuring them that each shield will look different. Offer support to those who may find it difficult to identify people or groups by prompting them to think about feelings such as kindness, encouragement or fairness that help them feel included. When finished, invite them to share part of their shield with a friend, small group or the whole class. Highlight that sharing is optional but can strengthen understanding and empathy. Finish by displaying the shields on a belonging wall or digital platform to celebrate diversity and connection.

Discussion Prompts

Use these prompts to open a thoughtful conversation about belonging, identity and the connections that help us feel part of a community.

- What does belonging feel like for you?
- Which people or places help you feel most connected?
- Which values on your shield matter most to you and why?
- What helps you feel included in this setting?
- How can we help others feel that they belong?

Extension or Adaptation Options

For younger children, use simple templates or support them to create a belonging picture instead of a shield, making the activity more visual and accessible. Older children may extend the task by writing a short reflection or giving a brief presentation on how belonging influences their motivation, confidence and wellbeing. In one-to-one or small group work, the shield can be used as a conversation tool to explore supportive relationships and personal values in more depth. As a whole class create a shared 'Coat of Arms' that represents the group's collective values such as respect, kindness and courage reinforcing a sense of community and belonging.

Activity: Kindness Challenge Calendar

Purpose

This activity helps children recognise how small, intentional acts of kindness strengthen resilience, belonging and emotional safety. By engaging with simple daily or weekly challenges, they experience how positive actions influence mood, connection and the overall climate of their education setting. The aim is to support kindness becoming a consistent habit that nurtures empathy, respect and inclusion.

Instructions

Begin by exploring what kindness looks, sounds and feels like within your setting. Invite children to share real examples, highlighting both everyday actions and the feelings they create. Reinforce that kindness is an attitude as well as a behaviour. Work together to create a visible kindness challenge calendar using a poster, whiteboard or printed template. Agree one achievable and meaningful act of kindness for each day or week. These might include offering encouragement, thanking someone who helped, including someone new in a game or acknowledging a friend's effort.

Display the calendar and encourage participation from everyone, including adults to model consistency. As challenges are completed, mark them off and capture brief notes or observations. Build in a short reflection at the end of each day or week and ask what happened, how they responded and what impact these actions had on the atmosphere, cooperation and overall energy of the group. Keep reflections warm, encouraging and solution focused to help embed kindness as part of everyday practice.

Discussion Prompts

To deepen reflection and encourage meaningful conversation, use the following prompts to explore how kindness and effort shaped their experiences this week.

- How did it feel to be kind or to have someone be kind to you this week?
- Did you notice any changes in how the group felt or got along?
- Which acts of kindness made the biggest difference and why do you think that is?
- How can we remember to be kind every day even when things feel hard?
- What does it look like in our group when we praise someone for trying, not just for being good at something?

Extension or Adaptation Options

Use picture cues for younger children to help them understand each kindness challenge and recognise what the actions look like in real life. Older children can be invited to co design the challenges, lead reflections or suggest ideas that feel meaningful to them. Journalling or drawing can be added for small groups or one-to-one sessions to help children think more deeply about how kindness affects their feelings and relationships. Share the calendars with families to encourage kindness at home or link the activity to PSHE, Citizenship or Character Education to highlight how kindness contributes to a positive community.

Activity: Ripple Wall of Kindness

Purpose

This activity supports children to recognise kindness as a practical resilience strategy. By noticing and offering small, positive actions they strengthen empathy, build connection and contribute to an environment where everyone feels valued. The 'Ripple Wall' becomes a visible reminder that everyday kindness benefits both the giver and the receiver.

Instructions

Begin by introducing the idea of ripples on water one small action can spread far beyond its starting point. Explain that kindness works in the same way, shaping how those around us feel and how communities' function. Create a simple display using concentric circles and provide each with a small card or paper circle and ask them to write one act of kindness or optimism they can carry out today. Offer examples such as including someone who seems on the edge of a group, offering help without being asked, thanking an adult who has supported them or choosing to speak gently when feeling frustrated. Invite them to add their circles to the display, expanding the ripple pattern with each contribution. As the wall grows, pause to reflect with the group on how these small actions, when combined, create a more compassionate atmosphere. Reinforce that the 'Ripple Wall' is a living display and encourage regular additions so it becomes part of the rhythm of the setting.

Discussion Prompts

Use these prompts to spark a reflective discussion on how everyday kindness shapes our feelings, relationships and resilience.

- How can small acts of kindness change the way we feel during the day?
- What happens when we notice and appreciate the things others do?
- When is being kind the most difficult and what helps us choose kindness anyway?
- Can you think of a time when someone's kindness really helped you?
- How might being kind help us when things feel tough or upsetting?

Extension or Adaptation Options

Use visual prompts or pre-written examples for younger children to help them think of simple acts of kindness they can offer. Older children may extend the activity by keeping journals or creating digital kindness ripple boards to track how their actions affect others over time. In one-to-one sessions the activity can be adapted into a kindness diary or a gratitude chain, giving them a more personal way to reflect on their actions and feelings. Settings may also choose to appoint kindness ambassadors, those who help promote positive behaviour across the group or link the activity to PSHE, citizenship or social responsibility lessons to embed kindness as an important resilience skill.

Activity: The Power of Yet!

Purpose

This activity helps children recognise that setbacks are a natural part of learning and that progress grows from effort, curiosity and self-belief. By introducing the idea of yet, they begin to shift from "I can't" to "I'm on my way", strengthening perseverance, emotional regulation and a shared culture where progress is valued as much as achievement.

Instructions

Begin with a short conversation about what happens when we add the word yet to a challenge. Explain that saying, "I can't do this yet", leaves room for growth and signals that developing a skill takes time. Offer a few relatable examples such as managing frustration, learning complex spellings or mastering a practical skill. Provide each with a speech bubble template; ask them to write one thing they feel they "can't do yet" inside the bubble. Around the outside, invite them to add words, actions or supports that could help them move forward. Encourage a range of ideas such as practising regularly, breaking tasks into steps, asking for guidance or learning from mistakes. Once completed, gather the bubbles to create a shared display titled 'The Power of Yet'. Encourage everyone to explore the display, noticing common strategies and the courage it takes to name an area for growth.

Conclude with a brief reflection on how changing our words can influence confidence, motivation and resilience.

Discussion Prompts

Use these prompts to explore how adopting a yet mindset can boost confidence, resilience and motivation during challenging moments.

- How does adding the word 'yet' change the way a challenge feels?
- How can noticing small steps help you feel more confident over time?
- What words or phrases help you keep going when something is hard?
- Can you think of something you once couldn't do yet but can do now?
- How could you use the idea of yet to encourage someone else?

Extension or Adaptation Options

Younger children may prefer drawing rather than writing their yet statement, making the activity more accessible and creative. Older children could extend the task by adding a brief action plan that shows the steps they will take to move forward. In one-to-one sessions, you can link the speech bubble to a personal target or support plan, helping them connect the idea of yet to something meaningful in their daily learning. Small groups or alternative provision settings may enjoy creating digital versions to build a virtual wall of progress that can be revisited over time. Families can also contribute their own bubbles, helping to reinforce the shared language of yet at home and strengthen the connection between education setting and family.

Activity: The "I Wonder . . ." Story

Purpose

This activity supports children to recognise curiosity as a resilience-building response when they meet uncertainty or challenge. By exploring a simple story and practising "I wonder . . ." statements they learn how curiosity can soften fear, increase confidence and strengthen their ability to adapt.

Instructions

Begin by acknowledging that feeling unsure is part of being human and explain that while fear can keep us safe, it can also hold us back. Curiosity, however, invites us to pause, think and move forward with greater control. Share a short, age-appropriate story or brief video clip showing a character facing something unfamiliar and choosing to explore rather than avoid it. This might involve starting at a new setting, joining a group or attempting a new activity. Some examples to use are *Inside Out* (Pixar), *Kung Fu Panda*, The Young Woman and the Sea (Disney), *The Dot* by Peter H. Reynolds, *Giraffes Can't Dance* by Giles Andreae.

After watching or reading, guide the group to notice what shifted when the character became curious. Highlight how "What if this goes wrong?" can become "I wonder what might happen if I try." Introduce the "I Wonder . . ." tool and model a few statements aloud, such as "I wonder what strengths I could use here" or "I wonder who might support me." Invite them to create their own statements linked to a real situation they are currently facing or anticipating. Provide time for them to record one chosen statement on paper or in journals. Encourage them to keep this visible as a reminder of how curiosity can help regulate emotions and open up options in challenging moments.

Discussion Prompts

Use these prompts to explore how curiosity can ease uncertainty, open up new possibilities and support clearer thinking in challenging moments.

- What was the character unsure or worried about?
- What changed when the character became curious instead of scared or stuck?
- How can being curious help us think clearly or solve problems?
- Can you think of a time when you felt unsure and how being curious might have helped you?
- How could using "I wonder . . ." help you next time something feels difficult or new?

Extension or Adaptation Options

Use picture books or simple role play activities for younger children to help them understand curiosity through characters and stories. Older children can take the idea further by writing short reflections or exploring how curiosity can change the way they approach challenges. In one-to-one or alternative provision settings personal stories, photos or scenario cards can be used to make the activity more relatable and support them in expressing their thoughts. You can also create an 'I wonder wall', where they add their own "I wonder . . ." questions over time, helping curiosity become a shared, everyday practice in the setting.

Activity: Three Good Things

Purpose

This activity supports children to build everyday resilience by intentionally noticing and reflecting on positive experiences. By practising gratitude, they begin to balance challenge with appreciation, strengthening emotional regulation and helping them recognise the role of their own actions, choices and relationships in shaping wellbeing.

Instructions

Introduce the activity by explaining that human brains often prioritise threats and difficulties. While this is natural, it can make it hard to spot what is going well; emphasise that resilience grows when they learn to hold both difficulty and hope in view. Define good things as small, positive moments from the day or week, a brief success, a kindness shown or received, enjoyment of an activity or persistence during something challenging. Model the process by sharing your own three good things, demonstrating that size or significance is not important - the act of noticing is what builds resilience.

Invite children to quietly think back over their day and identify three good things and ask them to record each one by writing or drawing in a journal, on paper or digitally. After each entry encourage a short note exploring why it happened, for example, "Because I asked for help", "Because I kept practising" or "Because someone included me". This helps them begin to link positive outcomes with effort, support and meaningful choices. Where appropriate, provide time for sharing one good thing with a partner or small group. For those who find it difficult to identify positives, gently support them to notice small but genuine moments, such as feeling welcomed, completing a task or taking a brave step.

Discussion Prompts

Use these questions to help them think about noticing good moments and practising gratitude.

- How did it feel to think about the good things from today?
- What part of this was easy and what part was a bit tricky?
- How do your feelings change when you focus on positive moments?
- How might remembering good things help you when you feel stressed or worried?
- How could sharing your gratitude help someone else feel good too?

Extension or Adaptation Options

Use visual prompts, a shared gratitude wall or a collaborative good things board to help younger children recognise positive moments together and build a sense of community. Older children may enjoy creating ongoing gratitude journals, digital reflections or more creative expressions such as letters, artwork or poetry that capture their good moments. In one-to-one sessions, simple conversations or using photographs can help make the activity easier and more personal. Families may also choose to take part by creating a gratitude week at home, strengthening the connection between setting and home.

Connecting the Learning

Developing a positive and realistic outlook is not an isolated skill but a foundational strand of resilience that shapes how children experience challenge, effort and change. Throughout this unit, optimism has been presented as a balanced way of seeing the world, one that allows hope and difficulty to sit alongside one another. When children are supported to notice what is going well, to recognise their own strengths and to feel a genuine sense of belonging, they are more able to approach setbacks with curiosity rather than fear, and persistence rather than avoidance.

For education settings, this work is deeply relational. Children learn optimism through what they experience repeatedly, adults who notice effort, name progress, validate emotions and create environments where mistakes are treated as part of learning rather than evidence of failure. These everyday interactions shape internal beliefs about capability, safety and possibility. Over time, a positive and realistic outlook strengthens emotional regulation, motivation and confidence, all of which are essential when children are required to learn under pressure or navigate uncertainty.

However, mindset alone is not enough. While optimism helps children believe that challenges can be managed, resilience is fully realised when belief is matched with practical skills. As children grow more hopeful and self-aware, they also need support to recognise stress responses, understand emotional signals and apply strategies that help them cope when emotions rise or situations feel overwhelming.

Unit 8 builds directly on this foundation. It moves from how children think about challenge to what they can do when challenge occurs. By introducing structured coping strategies and emotional regulation tools, the next unit supports children to act on the hope developed here, turning positive outlook into practical resilience. Together, these units reinforce a core message: resilience is strengthened through both mindset and action, supported by relationships, consistency and environments where children feel safe enough to try, reflect and grow.

Unit 8
Teaching Effective Coping Strategies

What this unit covers:

- Build everyday coping skills by identifying stressors, noticing triggers, and choosing helpful responses.
- Practise emotional regulation and resilient thinking using the 4-Step Resilience Building Framework and Zones of Regulation.
- Complete practical reflection and creative tasks such as coping toolkits, reframing tasks, choice scenarios, reflection prompts and creative boards.

Introduction

Coping strategies are best understood as everyday skills that can be taught, practised and strengthened, rather than tools reached when a crisis occurs. When children begin to see coping as part of daily life, they start noticing the small decisions that either support their wellbeing or make situations feel harder. This aligns with a well-established principle in education, emotional resilience grows through consistent repeated practice (Masten, 2014). Resilient thinking evolves through repeated encounters with constructive emotional habits. Over time, coping becomes embedded in the culture of the education setting a shared vocabulary of noticing, naming and managing emotions that enables them to stay engaged, even when learning presents challenges.

Adults play a pivotal role in helping children build these skills. Research continues to highlight the value of emotionally attuned adults who model calmness, curiosity and reflective problem-solving, offering a protective buffer when stress arises (Zimmer-Gembeck & Skinner, 2011). When adults show how they navigate their own emotions by pausing before responding, reframing a frustration or simply acknowledging when they need a moment, they provide children with a clear, accessible plan. This modelling reinforces the idea that resilience is not about suppressing feelings but about responding to them thoughtfully and with intention. Through reliable routines, strong relationships and an environment where seeking help is normalised, they learn that coping is a shared process. They come to understand that

DOI: 10.4324/9781003409632-9

resilience develops through guided practice, honest conversations and the reassurance of adults who support them every step of the way.

The Importance of Developing Coping Strategies

Helping children to develop effective coping strategies is a vital aspect of emotional resilience and overall wellbeing. Life often presents challenges and the ability to respond to these challenges with flexibility, optimism and perseverance determines how successfully they can thrive both in and beyond the classroom.

Research consistently highlights that coping is not a single skill but a combination of emotional, cognitive and behavioural responses that help children manage situations they experience as stressful (Lazarus & Folkman, 1984; Compas et al., 2017). This work distinguishes between problem-focused coping, which involves taking practical steps to address the source of stress, such as breaking a task into smaller parts or seeking support, and emotion-focused coping, which supports the regulation of feelings in the moment through strategies such as calming breaths, grounding techniques or reframing unhelpful thoughts. Together, these complementary approaches provide children with a flexible toolkit for responding to pressure with greater awareness, adaptability and control.

Children who develop effective coping strategies are better equipped to regulate emotions, maintain relationships and stay engaged in learning despite setbacks. These strategies can be learned, practised and strengthened over time through consistent modelling by adults and by creating opportunities for reflection and self-awareness. In classroom settings, this means moving beyond directing them to "calm down" or "get on with it" and instead teaching the specific skills that enable them to regulate emotions, solve problems and rethink unhelpful responses. Once they understand what triggers stress, the next step is learning how to respond in ways that support rather than undermine their wellbeing. Developing adaptive coping involves practising alternative responses and applying them independently.

Recognising Stressors and Emotional Triggers

All children experience situations, interactions or comments that heighten stress or discomfort. Supporting them to identify these triggers enables a clearer understanding of emotional responses and opens the door to more deliberate coping choices. The 4-Step Resilience Building Framework provides a straightforward method for helping them recognise stressors, interpret their reactions and develop more balanced responses under pressure.

The 4-Step Resilience Building Framework

The 4-Step Resilience Building Framework offers a simple, structured approach to helping children understand their emotional experiences and develop practical coping strategies they can use in everyday situations. By breaking the process into four manageable stages, the framework enables them to recognise what triggers their stress, reflect on their current responses and develop healthier alternatives.

Step 1: Identify Stressors

Support them to recognise and name the specific situations, people or triggers that cause them stress. Developing this awareness is the foundation for managing emotional responses effectively.

Step 2: Understand Current Responses

Guide them to explore how they typically react when faced with these stressors. This includes recognising unhelpful patterns such as avoidance, anger or withdrawal and understanding the impact of these responses on themselves and others.

Step 3: Create Alternative Responses

Work with them to develop and practise more constructive coping strategies. This may include problem solving, relaxation techniques, positive self-talk or seeking support. The focus is on expanding their emotional toolkit to handle pressure in healthier ways.

Step 4: Apply and Maintain Coping Skills

Provide ongoing opportunities for them to apply their new strategies in real-life situations. Reinforce progress through reflection, feedback and regular practice to ensure coping skills become embedded and sustainable over time.

The Zones of Regulation

Developed by Leah Kuypers (2011, 2024), the Zones of Regulation framework provides a simple system to recognise and manage their emotions. It categorises feelings, energy levels, and states of alertness into four coloured zones:

- Blue Zone: Sad, tired, or bored.
- Green Zone: Calm, focused, or happy
- Yellow Zone: Frustrated, worried, or silly.
- Red Zone: Angry, elated, or terrified

Teaching them to identify which zone they are in and to use specific strategies to regulate each zone builds self-awareness and emotional literacy. Strategies may include breathing exercises, movement breaks, journalling or positive self-talk. This process becomes internalised, enabling them to independently regulate their emotions and behaviour to support their goals and wellbeing.

Practical Ways to Teach Effective Coping Strategies

The following activities last between 20 and 40 minutes and are designed for children aged 7 to 14, with adaptations made as needed for younger or older children. Each activity is structured under the following headings, Purpose, Instructions, Discussion Prompts, and Extension or Adaptation. It is important to maintain emotional safety by ensuring that all contributions are respected and valued and by reinforcing that resilience grows through experience and reflection rather than through perfection.

Activity: My Resilience Toolkit

Purpose

This activity supports children to recognise their personal strengths and gather practical strategies that help them regulate emotions and sustain focus during demanding moments. It reinforces the idea that resilience develops through awareness, deliberate choices and repeated practice.

Instructions

Begin by acknowledging that everyone experiences pressure and that resilience is about recognising what helps them regain a sense of control when emotions feel difficult. Provide paper, notebooks or digital tools, along with colouring materials and display a few simple examples such as breathing cards, grounding techniques or supportive phrases. Encourage them to take their time and think honestly about what genuinely helps them feel steady, calmed or more in control. Offer prompts such as slow breathing, stretching, listening to music, talking to a trusted adult, using a sensory object, taking a movement break or repeating a reassuring phrase.

Invite them to choose the strategies that work for them and record these in any format that feels comfortable. Some may prefer drawing or creating symbols, others might choose audio recordings, photographs or a short written list. Reinforce that there is no right or wrong way to develop their toolkit. Support them to gather their ideas into a personal journal, folder or digital file and add a title such as 'My Resilience Toolkit', along with a brief statement about why these strategies matter to them. Offer the opportunity for anyone who wishes to share one or two of their chosen tools with the group. Remind them that the toolkit is personal and sharing is entirely voluntary.

Discussion Prompts

Use the following questions to help them reflect on how they recognise rising emotions and encourage them to choose the strategies that work best.

- What helps you the most when your feelings start to feel big or tricky?
- How can you tell when it's a good time to use something from your toolkit?
- What helps you focus or feel calmer when you're learning or paying attention?
- What could help you remember to use your tools during the day?

Extension or Adaptation Options

Younger children may benefit from visual aids such as symbols or pictures, they can extend the activity by setting personal goals, recording their responses or adding reflections within wellbeing journals or digital portfolios. In one-to-one sessions the toolkit can support emotional literacy conversations, while groups may enjoy creating a shared resilience wall. Families can also be invited to share ideas or complete linked activities at home to increase consistency between home and the education setting and reinforce the same language and strategies.

Activity: Best, Worst, Realistic

Purpose

This activity helps children recognise how their thinking patterns shape their emotional responses and choices. By exploring different possibilities, they learn to steady their thoughts, reduce anxiety and approach challenges with greater clarity and self-control.

Instructions

Introduce the idea that uncertainty can lead them to anticipate the most worrying outcome, a common cognitive response during stress. The 'Best, Worst, Realistic' framework helps them examine these thoughts and shift towards a more balanced assessment. Explain each component clearly and encourage them to work steadily, contributing honestly and reflecting on how their thinking changed as they identified the most realistic outcome. Briefly outline each part:

- Best Case: What is the most positive outcome we can imagine?
- Worst Case: What is the most difficult or worrying outcome we fear?
- Realistic: Based on past experience and current facts, what is most likely to happen?

Invite them to work in pairs or small groups, offer a relatable scenario or encourage them to choose one that feels meaningful to them. Ask each group to record their ideas under the three headings. Once groups have completed their lists, bring everyone together and ask them to notice any shift in how they felt as they moved towards identifying the realistic outcome; highlight that this step often brings a sense of relief and perspective.

Discussion Prompts

Use these questions to help them think about how their thoughts and feelings changed during the activity and how this strategy can help when things feel difficult.

- What did you notice about your thoughts when you went from the worst case to the realistic one?
- How did your feelings change as you worked through the activity?

- What helped you decide what was actually realistic?
- How could this way of thinking help you when you feel worried, stuck or unsure what to do next?

Extension or Adaptation Options

Use visuals such as emotion faces, coloured cards or simple objects to support younger children in recognising and naming their thoughts and feelings. Older children may benefit from extending the activity through journal reflections, digital wellbeing logs or short goal-setting prompts. In one-to-one or small-group sessions link the framework to real concerns they may have, such as moving to a new class, friendship worries or upcoming changes. Offering families a simple take-home template or prompt card can help strengthen continuity between home and the education setting and encourage consistent language and strategies.

Activity: The Choice Challenge

Purpose

This activity is designed to help children recognise that while circumstances may feel overwhelming, they retain the power to choose their response. This understanding strengthens emotional regulation, nurtures a sense of agency and supports the development of resilient thinking in everyday situations.

Instructions

Begin by explaining that everyone has choices, even when a situation feels difficult or unfair. Emphasise that the choices they make can shape both how they feel and what happens next. Share a few examples, such as "When you feel frustrated, you might choose to shout, take a breath, ask for help or step away for a moment."

Invite them to think about a recent situation they found challenging. Ask them to describe or write about it using the following prompts:

- What happened?
- What choices were available to you?
- What did you choose to do?
- What might have happened if you had chosen differently?

Support them to notice the connection between their choices, the outcome and how they felt afterwards. For those who find this difficult, begin by talking through a shared or imaginary example together. Reinforce the message that pausing before reacting is a sign of strength, not weakness and remind them that every new situation offers another opportunity to make a helpful choice.

Discussion Prompts

Use these questions to help them think about the choices they can make when things feel tough and how those choices can change how they feel and what happens next.

- How does it feel to know that you always have some control over what you do next?
- Which choices help you feel calmer, safer or more in control?
- Can you think of a time when making a good choice helped the situation turn out better?
- What could help you remember to pause and think before you react next time?
- How might your choices affect how other people feel or behave around you?

Extension or Adaptation Options

With younger children, use storybooks, puppets or simple drawings to explore the choices characters make in different situations. Pause the story to ask what the character could do next, what choice might help most and how different choices could change how the character feels or what happens. Older children may prefer journalling, group discussion or scenario-based conversations focused on real-life situations such as friendship challenges, disagreements or peer pressure. To strengthen links between home and the education setting, encourage families to have short, everyday conversations about choices, such as how they respond to frustration, disappointment or change.

Activity: Change Your Words

Purpose

The aim of this activity is to support children in recognising how their inner voice shapes their confidence, emotions and responses to challenge. By learning to reframe unhelpful thoughts into constructive, realistic alternatives, they strengthen emotional regulation, develop self-belief and build everyday resilience.

Instructions

Introduce the idea that internal thoughts influence confidence, emotions and behavioural responses. Explain that with practice they can adjust unhelpful thoughts and replace them with more constructive alternatives. This reframing supports persistence and helps them engage more effectively with challenging tasks. Begin by asking children to identify moments when their inner voice becomes particularly noticeable, such as when they feel worried, make a mistake or try something new. Use questioning to help them notice the tone of this voice: "Does it encourage you?" "Criticise you?" "Sound fair?"

Model the technique of reframing by sharing clear, relatable examples; for example, "I can't do this" could shift to "I can't do this yet", and "This is too hard" might become "This is hard, and I can take it step by step." Emphasise that reframing is not about pretending something is easy; it is about finding language that supports persistence. Next present several unhelpful statements on a board or screen. Ask pairs or small groups to create alternative versions that feel more balanced, kind or hopeful. Encourage them to draw on real situations where they felt stuck, using those moments to practise more helpful inner dialogue. Invite them to share their reframed statements and reflect briefly on how the revised wording alters their feelings or motivation.

Discussion Prompts

Use these questions to help them think about how changing their words can change how they feel and how confident they are to try again.

- What did you notice when you changed the words in your thought?
- Which versions felt more encouraging or easier to believe?
- How could different words help you feel braver or more willing to try again?
- When might you use this way of rewording a thought in your setting, at home or with friends?

Extension or Adaptation Options

Use visual prompts, simple role-play or character cards with younger children to help them practise changing unhelpful thoughts into more supportive ones. Older children may benefit from journalling, scenario-based discussions or short mindfulness activities that help them notice their thoughts before they begin reframing. Families can also be encouraged to model constructive and encouraging language at home to reinforce resilience and create consistent messages beyond the education setting.

Activity: I Was, I Am

Purpose

This activity helps children recognise how they have grown over time, strengthening self-belief, optimism and the understanding that change is possible. By noticing even small shifts, they build a clearer sense of agency and resilience, particularly when progress feels slow or uncertain.

Instructions

This activity encourages children to identify the strengths, values and sources of support that help them remain focused and motivated. By creating a visual representation of these elements, they develop a clear reminder of the factors that sustain their resilience during challenging periods. Provide each with a blank sheet divided into two labelled sections, 'I Was' and 'I Am'. Ask them to think back to a time such as the start of term, a recent challenge or a project and reflect on how they have changed since then. Encourage them to record at least three clear examples of progress and offer optional sentence starters such as "I was . . . I am now . . .".

If someone finds it difficult, guide them to notice micro-changes, for example "You've begun asking for help when things feel overwhelming." Invite them to share one or two examples with a friend or small group to foster connection and mutual encouragement. Finish with a short whole-group reflection focused on how naming personal progress can strengthen confidence, resilience and readiness for future challenges.

Discussion Prompts

Use these questions to help them think about the progress they've made and what has helped them grow along the way.

- What changes have you noticed in yourself since the start of this term?
- Which moment or example are you most proud of and why?
- What helped you make this change: was it a strategy you used, someone who supported you or a new way of thinking?
- How does noticing your progress make you feel about future challenges?

Extension or Adaptation Options

Use drawings, simple symbols or emotion faces with younger children to help them show their 'I Was' and 'I Am' statements. For older children, extend the activity by adding a third section 'I Want to Be', which helps them link their past growth to future goals and aspirations. In SEND/ALN or alternative provision settings, offer additional scaffolding, such as sentence starters, word banks, visual prompts or differentiated templates, and make it clear that giving verbal responses is a fully valid and supported option.

Activity: My Resilience Vision Board

Purpose

This activity supports children to explore what helps them stay grounded, motivated and hopeful. By creating a personal vision board, they clarify their strengths, values and sources of support, while developing a visual reminder of how they can recover and grow during challenging times.

Instructions

Begin by explaining that a vision board is a collection of images, words and colours that represent what strengthens us and keeps us going. Emphasise that this board is not about artistic ability but about capturing what resilience looks and feels like for each. Provide large sheets of paper or card, magazines, printed images, scissors, glue and coloured pens. Invite them to think about recent situations where they have shown determination, adapted to change or reached out for support. Encourage them to consider "Which qualities helped me?" "Who or what keeps me steady?" "What gives me hope?"

Ask them to choose images, phrases or symbols that reflect their strengths, aspirations, role models and moments of pride. They can also add their own key words or short affirmations. Support those who need reassurance by offering prompts such as "What helps you keep going when something is difficult?" or "What reminds you that you're capable?" Once completed, offer the option to share one or two elements with others. Finish by encouraging them to place their board somewhere visible so it can act as a daily reminder of their resilience and potential.

Discussion Prompts

Use these questions to help them think about what their board says about them and how it can support them when things feel challenging.

- What does your board show about what's really important to you?
- Which word or picture feels the most encouraging and why?
- How could this board help you when you're having a difficult moment?
- What similarities or differences did you notice between your board and other people's boards?

Extension or Adaptation Options

Provide pre-cut images, stickers or simple templates for younger children to help them build their boards more easily. Older children may choose to extend the activity by adding a short reflective journal entry that explains why they selected certain words or images. Digital versions can also be created using simple collage or mood board apps for those who prefer working on a device. In group settings they can work together to design a shared resilience wall that celebrates their collective strengths, values and supportive ideas.

Activity: Resilience Warriors

Purpose

This activity helps children consolidate their understanding of resilience by identifying the strategies that genuinely support them, recognising their progress and considering how they might encourage others. It strengthens self-awareness, confidence and empathy while embedding resilience as a shared value within the wider education setting.

Instructions

Position this activity towards the end of a resilience or wellbeing sequence so they can draw on a range of strategies already explored. Ask them to identify the approaches they use most consistently and the situations in which these strategies are most effective. Introduce the idea of becoming a 'Resilience Warrior', as an informal peer-support role in which they model constructive coping, empathy and positive communication. Provide reflection sheets or journals for them to record:

- The strategies they find most helpful.
- When and why they use them.
- How confident they feel applying these skills in different environments.

Facilitate a calm, structured discussion where they share examples of resilience in action. Encourage them to describe moments when they persisted, adapted or managed strong emotions. Introduce the idea of becoming a 'Resilience Warrior' who shows empathy, encouragement and active listening. Clarify that this is not a position of authority but a way of strengthening the community through kindness and supportive communication.

Discussion Prompts

Use these questions to help them think about the resilience skills they've been building, when they help most and how they can support others who might be finding things difficult.

- Which resilience strategies have helped you the most and why?
- When do you find it hardest to use these strategies? What helps you remember them?
- What qualities do you think a supportive 'Resilience Warrior' should have?
- How could you encourage another child who is feeling overwhelmed?

Extension or Adaptation Options

Younger children may prefer drawing, simple storytelling or using sentence starters to help them describe their resilience moments in a way that feels manageable and fun. Older children could take the activity further by creating a resilience pledge that outlines the strategies they want to keep using, or a peer support charter that explains how they will encourage and support others. Education settings might also choose to create a resilience wall to display strategies, pledges and success stories, helping the language, habits and celebrations of resilience stay visible across the whole community.

Connecting the Learning

As children learn to recognise their stressors, understand their emotional responses and practise constructive coping strategies, an important pattern begins to emerge. Coping depends on children being able to explain what they are feeling, make sense of their experiences and communicate their needs to others. Without the language to articulate emotions or the confidence to seek support, even well-practised strategies can remain difficult to apply in real situations.

This unit has emphasised that coping is not a single skill but a dynamic combination of emotional, cognitive and behavioural responses that develop through teaching, modelling and repeated practice. Through structured approaches such as the 4-Step Resilience Building Framework and the Zones of Regulation, children are supported to notice what triggers stress, reflect on habitual reactions and experiment with more helpful alternatives. The practical activities encourage self-awareness, agency and flexible thinking, enabling them to reframe challenges, regulate emotions and make more deliberate choices under pressure.

Importantly, these skills become most powerful when they are reinforced consistently within emotionally attuned environments. When adults model calm responses, reflective thinking and honest emotional language, children learn that resilience is built through supported practice rather than perfection. Over time, coping strategies become embedded habits that support learning, relationships and wellbeing across the wider education setting.

This growing capacity to manage internal experiences naturally leads to the next stage of resilience development. As children become more aware of what they feel and how they cope, they need opportunities to express those experiences clearly, listen to others and engage in supportive dialogue. Unit 9 therefore focuses on communication as a foundation for emotional literacy, exploring how effective expression, empathy and connection enable children to apply their coping skills confidently within relationships, learning and everyday life.

Unit 9
Developing Communication Skills

What this unit covers:

- Build resilience by naming emotions and communicating feelings clearly and respectfully.
- Strengthen relationships through active listening, empathy, validation and non-verbal awareness.
- Complete practical reflection and creative tasks such as feelings walls, silent scenes, listening ladders and 'I statement' practice.

Introduction

Communication is central to how children understand themselves, relate to others and manage the emotional demands of daily life. When communication is strong, confidence grows, relationships deepen and they feel connected to the adults who support them; when it weakens, even familiar situations can feel confusing or unsafe.

In education settings communication is not an optional skill but a core component of emotional literacy and resilience. Children do not simply acquire it through experience, they learn it through intentional teaching, consistent modelling and everyday interactions where adults demonstrate curiosity, empathy and respect. A shift in posture, a hesitant tone or a brief glance can reveal far more than words alone and when adults respond with understanding rather than judgement, children learn that their feelings are valid and manageable.

The language adults use plays a powerful role in shaping the communication culture of a setting. When adults communicate in ways that are warm, predictable and emotionally attuned, children are more likely to feel heard, valued and safe to express themselves. In contrast, rushed or dismissive responses, often unintentional, can quickly shut down communication and leave children feeling unseen or reluctant to share their voice.

This unit explores communication as a foundation of resilience; it introduces practical activities that help children express feelings, listen with empathy, make sense of non-verbal cues and engage in constructive dialogue. Over time these skills support them when emotions rise or relationships feel strained.

DOI: 10.4324/9781003409632-10

The Importance of Effective Communication

Communication is one of the most powerful tools we possess, it is the foundation of every relationship, every learning experience and every act of resilience. In education settings effective communication plays a pivotal role in helping children understand themselves, manage their emotions and build positive relationships with others.

In everyday interactions, children quickly learn that communication is about more than words alone. It is shaped by tone, timing and how safe it feels to respond. Research supports this view, with Hartley (2011) describing communication as the creation of meaning rather than the simple exchange of information. When communication breaks down, misunderstandings, conflict and emotional distress often follow. Equally, when communication is effective, children feel heard, valued and understood - essential ingredients in building resilience.

Resilience is not about being strong all the time, it is about recovering from difficulty. When a child can express their feelings clearly, listen to others and interpret non-verbal cues, they are better equipped to manage challenges, regulate emotions and seek help when needed. Many resilient children can identify at least one adult who consistently listens, believes in them and remains emotionally available during difficulty. This understanding is reinforced by longitudinal research, with Werner and Smith (1992) highlighting the importance of stable, supportive relationships with trusted adults as a key protective factor in children's resilience.

Understanding Effective Communication

Effective communication is rooted in empathy, understanding and genuine connection. It involves both the words we choose and the non-verbal signals that accompany them, including tone of voice, posture, facial expression and eye contact. In emotionally charged moments, children often respond less to what is said and more to how it is communicated. Foundational research by Mehrabian (1972), while widely debated and later expanded, highlighted the significant influence of tone and body language on how messages are received.

Resilience is not about avoiding difficulty, but about being able to recover from it. Communication provides a vital bridge between challenge and recovery. When children are supported to express their feelings, listen to others and interpret non-verbal cues, they are better able to regulate emotions, manage stress and seek help when needed. As Gilligan (2009) suggests, communication helps children make sense of experience and develop coping strategies. For example, resilience is being practised when a child learns to express frustration using words rather than aggression or to ask for support instead of withdrawing.

A helpful reflective lens from communication practice is the idea that the impact of communication is best understood through the response it creates. This perspective, often referenced within Neuro-Linguistic Programming (Bandler and Grinder, 1979), encourages adults to notice children's reactions and adjust their language accordingly. Small shifts in wording can make a meaningful difference. A statement such as "I'm really proud of you" may feel encouraging, or it may place value on adult approval, whereas language such as "You must feel really proud of yourself" can support internal validation and a growing sense of autonomy (Dweck, 2006). In practice, effectiveness depends less on adult intention and more on how the child experiences the message, reinforcing the importance of responsive and adaptable communication (Andreas and Faulkner, 1994).

Creating a Culture of Communication

Creating a culture of communication means ensuring that effective communication is embedded throughout the education setting environment. When adults consistently model positive communication, use restorative conversations after conflict and maintain a shared language of respect, they help build a resilient and emotionally safe learning culture.

Education settings can strengthen this, with check-ins to model emotional literacy, establishing classroom talk rules that emphasise listening, avoiding interruptions and respecting differences and adopting solution-focused language that shifts thinking from "What went wrong?" to "What can we do next?". They can also support them by encouraging peer mediation and restorative practices and by providing quiet, safe spaces for children who need time to pause and process before they communicate.

Practical Ways to Teach Effective Communication

The following activities last between 20 and 40 minutes and are designed for children aged 7 to 14, with adaptations made as needed for younger or older children. Each activity is structured under the following headings, Purpose, Instructions, Discussion Prompts, and Extension or Adaptation. It is important to maintain emotional safety by ensuring that all contributions are respected and valued and by reinforcing that resilience grows through experience and reflection rather than through perfection.

Activity: Feelings Wall

Purpose

The 'Feelings Wall' helps children develop a richer emotional vocabulary and recognise the full range of emotions they experience. By building a shared language for feelings, they strengthen their capacity to notice, express and regulate emotions core components of resilience in education settings.

Instructions

Identify a section of wall or display board to become the shared emotional space. Divide it into clear zones that reflect different levels of emotional intensity such as calm, steady, energised and overwhelmed. Begin with a brief conversation about why naming emotions matters, emphasising that words help us understand what is happening internally and choose helpful responses. Invite them to generate as many feeling words as they can. Encourage a balance of comfortable for example, hopeful, relaxed, proud and uncomfortable and emotions such as, tense, irritated, uncertain, then write each word on a separate card or sticky note.

Work together to sort the cards into the different zones, discussing where each emotion might sit and using colour coding to show variations in intensity. Arrange the display so that the progression between emotions is easy to see. Introduce a simple routine for using the 'Feelings Wall': this might be during daily check-ins, circle time or moments of transition. They place their name, initial or chosen symbol beside the word that best reflects how they feel. Model that all emotions are welcome and that noticing them is a strength, not a weakness. Regular use embeds emotional awareness and fosters a supportive climate.

Discussion Prompts

Use these prompts to explore how understanding and naming feelings can support emotional regulation, connection and empathy.

- Why is it good to know lots of different feeling words?
- How does saying a feeling out loud help you calm down?
- Which feelings are the hardest to talk about? Why?
- What can you do to help someone who is having a big feeling?
- How could the 'Feelings Wall' help everyone feel listened to and understood?

Extension or Adaptation Options

For younger children, include visual prompts such as pictures or colour-coded faces. Older children may benefit from access to a wider range of emotion words, including those that describe mixed or less familiar feelings, alongside opportunities to explore how emotions can change in strength and intensity over time. Families can also create a simple home version to support shared reflection. A portable 'Feelings Wall', using laminated cards or a keyring set, is particularly useful in one-to-one or alternative provision settings and can support regulation during transitions or moments of heightened emotion.

Activity: Big Feelings, Calm Responses

Purpose

Emotionally attuned responses are a foundation of resilience; when adults notice, name and accept the feelings of children, they learn that emotions are manageable rather than overwhelming. This activity helps practise emotionally validating language so they can strengthen connection, reduce escalation and support the development of self-regulation.

Instructions

Begin by introducing emotional validation to help recognise a feeling without judgement or correction. Stress that validation does not excuse unhelpful behaviour: it simply acknowledges the emotion driving it. Invite them to identify commonly used dismissive phrases they hear or catch themselves using, such as "You're fine" or "It's not worth getting upset about." Ask them to consider how these might affect their sense of safety, belonging and trust. Present a set of scenarios: for example, they get upset about feedback or feel angry after losing a game. Working in pairs or small groups, they take turns responding using emotionally validating language. Prompts might include "That sounds tough", "I can see this really matters to you", or "It's okay to feel cross, let's think about what could help."

Encourage careful attention to tone, facial expression and body language; guide observers to offer specific, constructive feedback on how well validation was conveyed and what helped the interaction feel calm and attuned. Bring the group together to reflect on what felt natural, what felt awkward and what small changes could make validation part of everyday interactions across education settings.

Discussion Prompts

Use these prompts to explore how emotions, communication and boundaries shape the way we connect with others during challenging moments.

- How does it feel when someone really listens to you and how can that help you behave differently?
- What can adults do to show they understand your feelings while still keeping clear rules?
- How can feeling stressed or upset make someone react differently when things are difficult?
- What kinds of body language help you feel safe and calm and what body language might accidentally make things feel worse?

Extension or Adaptation Options

For younger children, use visual supports such as emotion cards, pictures or simple emotion scales to help them recognise and name how they feel. With older children, the activity can be linked more explicitly to PSHE or wider wellbeing learning, exploring how emotions influence behaviour, relationships and decision-making. Also introduce discussing real-life scenarios, reflecting on how emotions show up differently in various contexts and considering strategies for managing strong feelings in a respectful and constructive way. In one-to-one sessions, practise using emotionally validating language with real-life situations that are meaningful to the child, allowing time for reflection and feedback.

Activity: Silent Scenes

Purpose

This activity supports children to explore how emotions, intentions and needs are communicated without words. By paying close attention to posture, facial expression and gesture, they strengthen empathy, emotional awareness and the ability to interpret social cues skills that underpin resilience and positive relationships.

Instructions

Invite them to work in groups of three to five and explain that each group will act out a brief everyday scenario using only non-verbal communication: no words, sounds or props should be used. Provide each group with a clear scenario prompt, for example offering comfort, asking for help, apologising, encouraging someone or inviting a friend to join in. Give groups several minutes to plan how they will communicate their scene through movement, expression and body language. Encourage them to consider "What emotion is at the heart of this scene?" "How might someone show this without speaking?"

When groups are ready, ask them to present their silent scene to the whole group. Invite everyone to observe carefully and guess what message is being expressed. After each performance, facilitate a short debrief exploring which non-verbal cues were most helpful, what could be made clearer and how different interpretations can arise.

Discussion Prompts

Use these prompts to think about how people communicate without words and how this can affect understanding.

- What was easy or tricky about acting without using any words?
- Which movements, facial expressions or actions helped show what was happening?
- Did anyone understand the scene in a different way? Why might that have happened?
- How can personal experiences change how someone understands body language?
- How can noticing body language help people get along better and stay calm in difficult moments?

Extension or Adaptation Options

With younger children, use simple and familiar scenarios such as losing a toy, sharing with a friend or waiting for a turn, keeping the focus on recognising basic emotions. With older children, introduce more complex situations and emotions, such as feeling left out, misunderstood or conflicted, and encourage discussion about how these might be shown through body language alone. In one-to-one or specialist settings, break each scene into smaller, manageable steps and provide prompts to support children in noticing and naming the emotions they observe. Families can also be encouraged to try silent scenes at home as a playful way to build connection, empathy and shared understanding through everyday interactions.

Activity: Listening Ladder

Purpose

This activity supports children to experience the emotional safety that comes from being listened to with genuine presence. Through structured practice they develop empathy, patience and clearer communication, which are the key building blocks of resilience. It also enables them to recognise how focused listening strengthens relationships and enhances their own emotional regulation.

Instructions

Begin by explaining that active listening means giving someone your full attention without interrupting, preparing a response or trying to solve their problem. Emphasise that the goal is simply to understand. Ask them to work in pairs; each will take a turn as a speaker and listener. Provide a timer or visual cue so the structure feels predictable and safe and invite the first speaker to talk for two minutes about a small worry, a recent experience or something that's been playing on their mind. The listener's role is to remain quiet, maintain a calm posture and show interest through eye contact or gentle nods; they should not offer advice or ask questions. When the timer ends, the listener summarises what they heard in one or two sentences, for example "You were nervous before the match but felt happy afterwards."

Pairs then switch roles and repeat the process. Once both turns are complete, allow time for shared reflection and reinforce that topics should remain comfortable to share and that both roles are equally important.

Discussion Prompts

Use these prompts to explore how active listening feels, what it looks like and how it can strengthen calm, respectful relationships.

- How did it feel when you could talk and no one interrupted you?
- What helped you stay focused while you were listening?
- What did you notice about your friend's face, body or voice?
- How can good listening help people stay calm and understand each other better?
- When might you use this kind of listening at your setting, at home or with friends?

Extension or Adaptation Options

Create a listening ladder poster highlighting key steps such as stillness, empathy and summarising. For younger children, keep the steps simple and visual, using pictures, symbols or colour coding to show each stage. For older children, introduce more detailed steps such as paraphrasing, asking clarifying questions and managing distractions. Use the activity in pastoral or one-to-one sessions to support emotional expression. Encourage families to try a short two-minute talk at home. Link the approach to curriculum tasks such as group projects, peer mentoring or reflective discussions in PSHE and English.

Activity: The Power of 'I'

Purpose

This activity helps children develop clear, respectful and emotionally aware communication. By practising 'I statements', they learn to express their feelings without blame, reduce reactive responses and strengthen resilience in everyday interactions at education settings, at home and with friends.

Instructions

Begin by inviting children to think about what people sometimes do when emotions run high. Record their ideas and use this as a starting point to discuss how quick, unfiltered reactions can escalate tension. Explain that the language we choose directly shapes how others respond and that 'I statements' offer a calm, assertive alternative. Introduce the structure I feel (emotion) when (situation) because (reason) and I would like (desired action or outcome). Highlight how this format encourages ownership of feelings rather than placing blame. Model examples, such as "You never listen to me!" versus "I feel overlooked when I'm not listened to." Ask the group which version feels easier to hear and why.

Display a small selection of unhelpful phrases and demonstrate turning one into an 'I statement' using the structure above. Then invite them to work in pairs or small groups to reframe each phrase. Encourage them to draw on real or imagined situations, for example, disagreements, feeling excluded or changes to plans made by friends. Support them to share their statements and discuss how tone, clarity and emotional impact shift when language becomes more constructive. Emphasise that 'I statements' do not minimise strong emotions; instead, they allow them to be honest, respectful and solution-focused.

Discussion Prompts

Use these prompts to explore how 'I statements' and thoughtful communication can make conversations calmer, clearer and more respectful.

- How does it change the message when you say "I feel . . ." instead of "You always . . ."?
- Why do you think people might listen better when you explain your feelings this way?
- When can blaming someone make a problem bigger instead of better?
- How can your tone of voice, your face and your body language change the way someone hears your message?

Extension or Adaptation Options

For younger children, simplify the 'I statement' structure and use visual supports to help them identify and name their feelings. Older children can apply the approach through brief role-plays, real-life scenarios or structured peer feedback, allowing them to explore how 'I statements' can support clearer and calmer communication in everyday situations. In one-to-one or restorative settings, build the use of 'I statements' into mentoring or support goals and practise them in small, carefully supported steps. This may include rehearsing responses to familiar situations or reflecting on recent interactions. Providing sentence starters, visual prompts and clear examples ensures the strategy remains accessible and helps all children use it with confidence and consistency.

Activity: Confidence Without Comparison

Purpose

This activity develops children's capacity to recognise their own progress, effort and personal strengths. By shifting emphasis from external approval to internal validation adults can nurture confidence, independence and a resilient sense of self. It also supports a reflective culture where emotional safety and self-awareness are prioritised.

Instructions

Introduce the activity by explaining that achievements often feel most meaningful when they understand why they matter to them. Invite children to recall a moment when they accomplished something important and to consider what made it satisfying. Briefly explore the difference between an adult telling them they have done well and them noticing this for themselves. Share several commonly used praise phrases, for example, "I'm proud of you" or "That's brilliant" and highlight how these place the focus on the adult's viewpoint. Then model how to reframe language to encourage internal reflection, using prompts such as, "What part of that went well for you?" or "How did you manage the difficult moments?"

Provide a flipchart or whiteboard and work together to collect additional reflective phrases. Ask pairs to choose familiar praise statements and rephrase them. Bring the group back together for a debrief and discuss when this approach can be included into everyday interactions during feedback, mentoring, restorative conversations or emotional regulation support. Reinforce that reflective questioning is not about removing warmth but about helping them grow confident in their own judgement.

Discussion Prompts

Use these questions to think about how noticing your own effort and progress can help you feel more confident and motivated.

- How does it feel if you only feel proud when someone else says "well done"?
- What feels different when you notice something you tried hard at or improved yourself?

- When can it be tricky to think about your own progress, and how could an adult help?
- How can kind, helpful feedback from others help everyone feel more confident and keep trying?

Extension or Adaptation Options

For younger children, use drawing, symbols or play-based prompts such as "Show me something you felt proud of today" to help them reflect in a concrete and accessible way. Older children may benefit from feelings scales, short weekly reflection journals or structured mentoring questions that support deeper thinking about progress, challenge and personal strengths.

In one-to-one work, link reflective prompts to personal goals, helping children notice small steps forward and build confidence over time. In group settings, introduce peer feedback using reflective phrasing, for example, "What did you notice about your contribution today?" or "What helped the group work well?" Families can also be offered a simple reflection sheet to encourage shared language and consistent reflection between home and the education setting, strengthening children's sense of continuity and support.

Activity: Shared Struggle

Purpose

This activity helps children use language that normalises struggle and reframes setbacks as a natural part of healthy learning. It encourages them to see difficulty as something safe, shared and valuable, strengthening their confidence, sense of emotional safety and willingness to keep going when tasks feel challenging.

Instructions

Prepare two contrasting sets of phrases, one list of fixed-mindset or dismissing statements often used with good intentions, for example, "Don't worry, this is easy" and a second list showing growth-oriented alternatives, for example "This can feel challenging at first. Let's work it out together." Begin by exploring how adults' words shape how children interpret success, difficulty and mistakes. Clarify that when we rush to reassure or gloss over challenge, children may learn that struggle is a sign they are "not good at something", rather than evidence that their brain is adapting and strengthening. Invite the group to examine each fixed-mindset phrase and ask them to consider how they might feel hearing it and what emotions, assumptions or pressures might be created.

Introduce the alternative phrases and discuss why they promote resilience. Highlight language that supports curiosity, for example "What might help next?", "You worked hard on that step", "You don't have to manage this alone." Briefly link to research showing that effort, error and practice build flexible neural pathways and problem-solving capacity. Finish by asking them to identify one phrase they will consciously replace this week and how they will include it in daily interactions.

Discussion Prompts

Use these prompts to think about how the words adults use can change how difficult things feel.

- How can the way an adult talks make something feel easier or harder?
- Are there any things adults say that can make you feel like giving up?
- What does it sound like when an adult stays calm, kind and helpful during a tricky moment?
- How can adults talk to you in ways that help you try your best and still feel safe and supported?

Extension or Adaptation Options

To extend this activity, create a shared resilience phrase bank for staff areas or family communication, highlighting examples of language that supports effort, problem-solving and persistence. Younger children can be invited to design posters that illustrate brain growing messages, helping them visualise how learning and effort work together. Older children may benefit from reflecting on a personal setback and identifying what helped them keep going, such as support from others, trying a different strategy or managing strong emotions. Adult development time can also be used to explore how adults' own self-talk, emotional regulation and language choices model resilient behaviour. Reflecting on how responses to pressure, mistakes or challenge are communicated helps ensure that adults consistently demonstrate the calm, flexible and reflective approaches they want children to develop.

Activity: Meet Your Inner Voice

Purpose

This activity supports children to notice the link between their thoughts, feelings and actions. By exploring their inner voice, they learn how self-talk can shape confidence, emotional regulation and resilience. The aim is to help them recognise helpful and unhelpful thought patterns and strengthen the caring voice that encourages them to keep going when facing challenges.

Instructions

Introduce the idea that everyone has an inner voice, the constant thoughts that can reassure, question or sometimes criticise. Explain that developing resilience begins with understanding these voices rather than judging them. Invite children to think about what their inner voice sounds like during difficult moments. Does it worry, encourage, doubt or guide? Provide a choice of creative mediums - drawing, writing or collage - to represent the different voices they notice. Encourage them to give each voice a name or character, such as 'The Critic', 'The Worrier', 'The Problem Solver' or 'The Faithful Friend'.

Once they have created their representations, ask them to identify which voices strengthen their confidence and which tend to interrupt it. Emphasise that all voices have a purpose and can be understood and managed. To finish, ask each to focus on their 'Faithful Friend' and write one supportive phrase they can use when facing a future challenge; reinforce that practising this voice builds resilience over time.

Discussion Prompts

Use these questions to help them think about their inner voice, how it affects their choices and how kind self-talk can help with challenges.

- What does the little voice in your head usually say when things feel difficult?
- How can you tell if that voice is helping you or making things feel worse?
- What kind, encouraging things might your 'Faithful Friend' voice say when you feel unsure, annoyed or overwhelmed?
- Can you think of a time when positive self-talk helped you do something tricky?
- How could using kind, supportive self-talk help a friend who is having a tough time?

Extension or Adaptation Options

For younger children, use puppets or familiar story characters to introduce the idea of different inner voices in a playful and accessible way. Acting out situations can help children recognise how thoughts influence feelings and choices. With older children, explore simple thought-reframing strategies, supporting them to practise turning unhelpful thoughts such as "I'll never get this right" into more supportive alternatives like "I'm still learning, and I can improve with practice." Families can also be encouraged to create a shared 'Faithful Friend' poster at home, helping to build a consistent, collective language of encouragement that supports confidence and resilience beyond the education setting.

Activity: What Would Captain Resilience Say?

Purpose

This activity supports children to practise perspective taking by imagining how a resilient role model might respond to everyday challenges. By stepping into someone else's shoes, they strengthen empathy, emotional regulation and reflective thinking, which are core components of resilience.

Instructions

Begin by introducing the idea that when challenges happen, it is easy for them to focus only on their own feelings. Perspective-taking helps us to pause, slow down our reaction and consider how a calm, resilient person might respond in the same situation. Create a shared model such as an imaginary 'Captain Resilience', who stays composed, notices their emotions and chooses helpful actions. With older children, invite them to select a real or fictional person they admire, for example, Marcus Rashford. Briefly explore what makes that person resilient and how they demonstrate courage, persistence or compassion.

Present a set of short, relatable scenarios, for example, "You are told to stop talking but feel annoyed", "The task feels too difficult" or "Someone pushes in front of you". Ask them, "What would your resilient role model say or do in this moment?" Provide speech or thought bubble templates for them to write or draw their responses. Model your own thinking aloud to show how a resilient inner voice sounds. Finish by asking them to identify one upcoming situation where they could try this perspective-taking strategy, helping them transfer the learning into everyday experiences.

Discussion Prompts

Use these questions to think about how imagining a positive role model can help with tricky situations.

- How might things feel different if you tried to see the situation like your role model would?
- What might your role model say to stay calm or keep going?
- When could this idea help you at school, with friends or at home?
- Can you think of a time when you saw someone handle a difficult situation really well?

Extension or Adaptation Options

Younger children may benefit from decorating a simple 'Captain Resilience' outline with supportive words or phrases that help them feel calm and confident during tricky moments. This visual reminder can be kept in the classroom or a personal folder for reassurance. Older children could create a resilient role model wall, showcasing positive role models and the phrases or strategies they might use when facing challenges, or write a short message from their role model offering guidance or encouragement. In one-to-one or small-group sessions, revisit the activity at a later point to reflect on how the strategy has been used in real situations. This might include discussing what worked well, what felt difficult and how the approach could be adapted next time, helping to strengthen transfer and build confidence over time.

Activity: Words That Build Confidence

Purpose

This activity supports adults to notice, reflect on and intentionally reshape the language they use with children. Everyday comments can either limit or strengthen individuals' resilience, influencing how they view challenge, effort and their own capacity to grow. By practising small changes in phrasing, adults can model persistence, encourage problem-solving and nurture a culture of resilient thinking across education settings.

Instructions

Begin by introducing the idea that the language children hear regularly shapes their beliefs about learning and coping with challenge. Briefly explain that messages emphasising effort, strategy and progress are linked to increased resilience and willingness to keep going when things feel tough. Present a familiar example, such as, "You're so clever," and ask the group to consider what this might imply about success and ability. Then share growth-oriented alternatives such as "You worked steadily on that task" or "You kept trying different ideas until something clicked." Next organise a structured reframing activity by providing pairs or small groups with a set of commonly used fixed statements, for example, "You're a natural", "Don't worry, it's easy", or "You're just not good at this." Ask them to rewrite each one so it recognises effort, strategy or perseverance.

Invite groups to share their reframed versions, capturing key phrases on a flipchart to create a shared resilient language wall. Finish by highlighting that subtle, consistent shifts in language can reinforce self-belief and support them to approach difficulty with greater confidence.

Discussion Prompts

Use these questions to think about how the words people use can help others feel confident and keep trying.

- When an adult says something like "You're so clever", what might that make someone think about things being easy or hard?
- How can kind or helpful words help someone keep going when something feels really tricky?
- What could change about the way people talk to each other to help everyone feel stronger and more confident?
- How could using positive, encouraging words make talking and working together at home easier?

Extension or Adaptation Options

Create a resilient language toolkit for adults that includes examples of supportive phrases, quick reference cards and simple scripts to encourage consistent, helpful language across the setting. These resources can be shared during staff meetings or training sessions to build a common approach. Use role-play with parents and carers to demonstrate how small changes in wording can make conversations feel calmer, more encouraging and more supportive at home. During one-to-one or small-group sessions, incorporate visual cue cards so children can choose or point to phrases that help them stay motivated and manage challenge when tasks feel difficult. This supports independence and helps reinforce resilient language in everyday interactions.

Connecting the Learning

Effective communication sits at the heart of emotional literacy and resilience. When children are supported to name feelings, listen with curiosity, interpret non-verbal cues and express themselves clearly, they develop far more than conversational skill. They gain a framework for understanding themselves, making sense of others and staying regulated when emotions run high. Throughout this unit, communication has been explored not as a simple exchange of words, but as a relational process that shapes identity, builds trust and supports recovery when things feel difficult.

Through intentional modelling, emotionally attuned responses and everyday practice, adults can turn ordinary interactions into powerful moments of learning. Skills such as validation, reflective questioning, perspective-taking and supportive self-talk help children feel seen and understood, while also strengthening autonomy and problem-solving capacity. As Riley (2019) highlights, trust grows through relationships, information and knowledge and effective communication brings these elements together in ways that help children feel safe enough to engage, reflect and try again.

As communication skills strengthen, so too does children's capacity to form and sustain positive relationships. Feeling heard makes connection possible, and connection provides the emotional safety that resilience depends upon. This leads naturally into the focus of the next unit, which explores how education settings can actively nurture supportive networks and a sense of belonging. Unit 10 builds on the communication foundations established here, examining how relationships with peers, adults and the wider community amplify resilience, confidence and wellbeing over time.

Unit 10
Building Supportive Relationships

What this unit covers:

- Identify trusted people, places and routines that help children feel safe, valued and ready to learn.
- Recognise what supportive relationships look and feel like, and how to seek and offer help.
- Complete practical reflection and creative tasks such as support-network mapping, safe-harbour drawings, feelings and behaviours charts.

Introduction

Strengthening children's resilience begins with strengthening their connections. While resilience is sometimes viewed as an individual skill, research and practice show that it grows within supportive relationships (Masten, 2014; Ungar, 2012). When children feel known, valued and included, they are better able to manage pressure, regulate emotions and stay engaged in learning.

In many education settings, difficulties with behaviour, confidence or wellbeing often trace back to a sense of disconnection. By contrast, when adults model warmth, consistency and empathy and when peers learn to support and include one another, children experience the predictable relationships that help them feel secure. These everyday interactions form the foundation for readiness to learn.

This unit explores practical ways adults can support children to recognise who is there for them, understand what safe and trustworthy relationships feel like and develop the skills needed to connect positively with others. The activities are inclusive and designed to sit within everyday practice. By embedding relational experiences across the setting, adults help create environments where belonging is expected and sustained, allowing resilience to take root and providing a secure foundation for the problem-solving work introduced in Unit 11.

DOI: 10.4324/9781003409632-11

The Importance of Building a Social Network

For many children, developing a strong social network is a key protective factor for emotional health, behaviour and overall wellbeing. A social network is more than a group of friends; it is a web of supportive relationships that provide guidance, empathy, practical help and a sense of belonging.

Children who feel connected to others are better able to cope with life's challenges. Research shows that these children tend to demonstrate higher levels of resilience, alongside lower levels of anxiety and depression (Werner and Smith, 2001). This reflects Bronfenbrenner's ecological systems theory (1979), which highlights how children are shaped by the interconnected environments around them, including family, education settings, peer groups and the wider community. When these systems are nurturing and joined up, children are more able to learn, adapt and thrive. When they are broken or inconsistent, coping becomes harder and emotional vulnerability increases.

Resilience is therefore rarely built in isolation. It grows within relationships that offer safety, perspective and encouragement, allowing children to experience challenges as shared rather than solitary. These everyday experiences of care and connection form what Masten (2014) describes as "ordinary magic", supporting positive adaptation even during periods of stress.

Strong social networks also support the development of emotional intelligence. Through supportive relationships, children build empathy, social awareness and the skills needed to manage relationships effectively (Collaborative for Academic, Social, and Emotional Learning [CASEL], 2020). As they learn to both seek and offer support, their sense of agency and belonging increases, strengthening confidence and self-belief. These experiences are central to psychological resilience, helping children feel capable, connected and able to persist when faced with difficulty (Bandura, 1997).

Practical Ways to Teach Building Supportive Social Networks

The following activities last between 20 and 40 minutes and are designed for children aged 7 to 14, with adaptations made as needed for younger or older children. Each activity is structured under the following headings, Purpose, Instructions, Discussion Prompts, and Extension or Adaptation. It is important to maintain emotional safety by ensuring that all contributions are respected and valued and by reinforcing that resilience grows through experience and reflection rather than through perfection.

Activity: The Balloon and the String

Purpose

This activity helps children understand how identity, confidence and trusted relationships work together to support resilience. The balloon represents their sense of self, while the string symbolises the secure connections that help them feel grounded, valued and able to take healthy risks.

Instructions

Begin by introducing the idea that they need both steadiness and space to grow. Explain that the balloon shows who they are and the string represents the people who help them stay steady when life feels challenging. Provide paper and drawing materials and ask them to draw a large balloon connected to a string. Inside the balloon invite them to write or illustrate words, images or symbols that reflect their interests, strengths, values and hopes for the future. Along the string, they should add the names or initials of people who help them feel safe, encouraged and cared for. This might include family, friends, trusted adults, community members or professionals. At the bottom of the string, ask them to draw a hand holding it, as a visual reminder of their secure base. When finished, offer time for sharing in pairs or small groups. Encourage them to explain what their balloon represents and how the people on their string strengthen confidence and emotional safety.

Discussion Prompts

Use these questions to guide reflection and help them explore how their support networks contribute to their sense of safety, confidence and resilience.

- Who helps hold your balloon steady when things feel uncertain?
- What do these supporters do that helps you feel safe or brave?
- How does having a secure base make it easier to try new things or cope with setbacks?
- Why is it good to have help and also try things by yourself?
- How might you show appreciation to those on your string?

Extension or Adaptation Options

Offer templates or picture cues to support younger children or those who benefit from additional structure. Older children may extend the activity into a short reflective journal entry exploring how their support networks influence their wellbeing, confidence or learning. As a group, create a collective wall of support to recognise and celebrate positive relationships within the setting. In one-to-one or SEND/ALN contexts, use the activity as a starting point for guided discussion about emotional safety, trusting relationships and individual strengths, adapting the pace and format to suit the child's needs.

Activity: Supportive Five

Purpose

To help children recognise the trusted adults who contribute to their sense of safety, belonging and resilience. By mapping out supportive people both within and beyond their education setting, they develop a clearer understanding of who they can approach for comfort, guidance or practical help, especially when under pressure.

Instructions

Introduce the idea that resilient individuals know when to seek support and who they can rely on. Explain that this activity will help children identify five trusted adults in their education setting and five in their home life. Once these people have been identified, help children understand that these are the adults they can go to when they face a challenge, need reassurance or want to share and celebrate successes.

Provide each child with a blank sheet of paper and ask them to place their hand on the page and carefully draw around it. Invite them to write the name of one trusted adult on each finger, encouraging them to think broadly, for example pastoral staff, teaching assistants, lunchtime supervisors, office staff or any adult who helps them feel safe or understood. Prompt them to consider the different types of support these adults offer, such as listening, helping them calm down, problem solving or simply being present.

Next, ask them to repeat the activity for trusted adults outside the setting, ensuring these individuals are known and approved by the parent or carer. Emphasise that trusted support can come from family members, neighbours, community leaders, coaches or longstanding family friends. Invite children to add colour, symbols or simple illustrations that represent the warmth and steadiness these adults bring. For those who struggle to name five adults, gently support them in identifying at least one and explore ways of strengthening connections over time.

Discussion Prompts

Use the following prompts to guide a reflective discussion about trust, support and community.

- What qualities make someone feel trustworthy or approachable?
- How do you know when it might be time to ask for help?
- How does it feel to recognise that you have people around you who care?
- In what ways can you offer support to others in your community?

Extension or Adaptation Options

Use pre-drawn templates or photographs of hands for younger children, alongside pictorial prompts of familiar adults. Older children may extend the task by creating a personal resilience map, linking trusted adults to different areas of their life such as learning, friendships, emotional support or hobbies. In one-to-one or small-group work, use the activity as a starting-point to explore support networks in greater depth, including when and how different adults can help. Families can be invited to continue the conversation at home, helping to strengthen shared understanding and consistency between home and education settings.

Activity: My Safe Harbour

Purpose

This activity supports children to recognise the people, places and routines that help them feel grounded, safe and emotionally regulated. Building this awareness strengthens their capacity to draw on protective factors when managing pressure, uncertainty or change.

Instructions

Introduce the idea that everyone needs moments, relationships and environments where they feel calm, cared for and steady. Explain the harbour metaphor: just as a harbour shelters a boat from rough seas, trusted people and familiar routines can offer protection when life feels challenging. Provide paper and colouring materials and ask them to create a drawing titled 'My Safe Harbour' and ask them to include:

- Inside the harbour: people, places and routines that help them feel secure, such as family members, trusted adults, pets, comforting activities or consistent daily habits.
- In the surrounding sea: any storms or challenges they may encounter, for example friendship problems, worries about tests, changes to routine, feeling left out.
- On the lighthouse: a reassuring message or affirmation that acts as a guiding light, such as "I can ask for help" or "I am not alone".

Encourage them to take their time, noticing how each element contributes to their sense of safety. When finished, invite voluntary sharing in pairs or small groups, focusing on what helps them remain settled during difficult moments. Ensure space for quiet reflection for those who prefer not to share. Respond to all contributions with warmth and validation and follow safeguarding procedures if sensitive information is disclosed.

Discussion Prompts

Use these questions to help them reflect on what makes their harbour feel safe and supportive.

- What makes your harbour feel cosy, calm or safe?
- Who helps you when things feel a bit stormy or difficult?
- How do your daily routines help you feel steady or focused?
- What could you do if one of your safe places or safe people wasn't there?
- How can you help others in our group or setting feel safe and welcome?

Extension or Adaptation Options

Use templates or picture cards to support younger children or those who benefit from visual prompts. Older children may develop their harbour into a short, written reflection, piece of artwork or simple digital design, exploring what helps them feel safe and steady. In one-to-one or small-group settings, use the harbour concept as a focus for guided conversation, allowing children to talk through their ideas at a pace that feels comfortable. As a wider community project, create a shared display celebrating sources of safety, connection and hope, helping to reinforce a culture of belonging across the setting.

Activity: Feel and Do

Purpose

To strengthen children's relational literacy by helping them recognise how supportive relationships contribute to resilience. By linking feelings to specific behaviours, they learn what helps them feel safe, respected and able to cope with challenges.

Instructions

Introduce the idea that resilient individuals often have a network of trusted people who help them feel grounded and understood. Explain that these relationships act as a protective buffer during stressful moments. Invite each child to think of someone with whom they feel comfortable. This may be a friend, family member or trusted adult.

Ask them to name the feelings this person brings out in them, for example, calm, hopeful, included or safe. This can be modelled with an example, such as "I feel supported by my friend because when I have a problem, they always listen to me and try to help."

Provide a simple two-column 'Feelings' and 'Behaviours' sheet. In the first column, children record the feelings they experience with this person. In the second, they identify what that person does to create those feelings, such as listening carefully, noticing when things are difficult, keeping confidence or showing patience.

Once completed, ask them to rate how safe or supported they feel with this person on a scale of 1 to 5. Reinforce that there are no right or wrong answers. The purpose is to help children understand emotional boundaries and recognise which relationships support their wellbeing. Ensure the task is approached gently, offering alternatives if anyone prefers not to focus on a specific person. If disclosures or concerns arise, follow the setting's safeguarding procedures.

Discussion Prompts

The prompts below are designed to encourage reflection on how we treat others, how others treat us and the support we can seek when needed.

- What do people do that helps you feel safe, respected or cared about?
- How do you feel inside when someone is unfair or unkind to you?
- What can you do to be kind and fair to other people?
- Who can you go to for help when life feels tricky or tough?

Extension or Adaptation Options

Use drawings, symbols or colour to support younger children or those who find written tasks challenging. Older children may extend the activity by exploring themes of boundaries, reciprocity and trust, including how these apply within online and digital relationships. As a group, create a shared display titled 'What helps us feel safe?' to highlight positive behaviours and supportive actions. Families can also be invited to discuss the completed sheet at home, helping to reinforce shared understanding and consistent messages about safety, respect and support across settings.

Activity: Cooperative Feeding

Purpose

To strengthen cooperation, empathy and shared problem solving by allowing children to experience how relying on others can build trust and resilience. The activity helps them recognise that accepting and offering help are equally valuable skills within any supportive environment.

Instructions

Introduce the activity as a practical exploration of teamwork when faced with a simple but meaningful challenge. Explain that the focus is on noticing how the group communicates, adapts and encourages one another. Before beginning, check all dietary, sensory and cultural needs. Seat the group around a table and provide each child with a small bowl of cereal, or an agreed alternative and a spoon. Ask them to place one arm behind their back and hold the spoon with the other, explaining that they may not use the spoon to feed themselves.

Introduce the challenge: "Your task is to work out how you might still enjoy your cereal." Allow time for them to think, experiment and negotiate possible solutions. Resist the temptation to guide too quickly; the learning comes from the process. Most groups discover that feeding one another is the most effective solution. Observe how they communicate, adapt their approach and support those who hesitate. Offer reassurance to anyone uncomfortable with close contact or food-based tasks and provide alternatives such as offering sips of water in cups. Throughout, acknowledge examples of cooperation, careful listening and shared decision making.

Discussion Prompts

Use these prompts to explore what the activity teaches about trust, cooperation and accepting support from others.

- How did it feel to depend on others for something you usually manage alone?
- What helped you trust your friend or group?

- What made cooperation easier or more challenging?
- Why might accepting help be just as important as offering it?

Extension or Adaptation Options

Use dry snacks for younger children to reduce mess and place greater emphasis on turn-taking and cooperation. Older children may benefit from linking the activity to experiences of leadership, team sports or collaborative projects, helping them reflect on how trust and communication support shared success. In therapeutic or alternative settings, the activity can be adapted to explore the idea of feeding others through encouragement, reassurance and inclusion rather than physical food. Families can also recreate a simple version at home, reinforcing shared responsibility, cooperation and mutual support in everyday situations.

Activity: Keep the Ball Moving

Purpose

This activity helps children experience how shared focus, communication and calm perseverance support resilience. Through a simple physical challenge, they explore how they adapt when the pressure increases, how they stay regulated when things go wrong and how they draw on others to keep going.

Instructions

Explain that the group's aim is to keep each ball travelling smoothly around the space without letting it stop or fall. Begin with one ball and invite them to stand in a circle or across two lines, ensuring everyone can see one another clearly. Ask them to establish a steady rhythm of gentle throwing and catching. Once this feels good, gradually introduce additional balls, varying size and weight to increase the demands on coordination and attention. Encourage them to use eye contact, open body language and clear non-verbal signals to show they are ready. Remind them to stay calm, avoid calling over one another and keep movements predictable. If a ball is dropped or the pattern breaks down, pause briefly. Invite a quick reset: "What happened?" "What helped?" "What might they try next?" Keep the tone light and constructive. Continue adding balls until the group must rely on shared awareness, adaptability and encouragement to maintain the flow.

Discussion Prompts

The following prompts can be used to reflect on how communication, cooperation and emotional regulation supported the group during the activity.

- What helped you keep the balls moving without stopping?
- How did you let other people know you were ready?

- What did you notice about how well everyone worked together when the game got harder?
- How did you feel when something went wrong and what helped you get back on track?
- What can this game teach us about staying calm and working together when things get tricky?

Extension or Adaptation Options

Use larger, slower moving balls for younger children or those who need additional support, allowing more time to track and respond. Older children or more confident groups may enjoy variations such as increased distances. In one-to-one or home contexts, adapt the task to a simple back-and-forth throw, using the activity as an opportunity to focus on encouragement, noticing effort and reflecting on what helped the interaction go well. This activity links well to Physical Education, PSHE and wellbeing work, particularly in relation to communication, emotional regulation and resilience.

Activity: The Laugh Ladder

Purpose

To support children in recognising humour as a resilience tool that can ease emotional tension, strengthen relationships and promote a sense of balance. Laughter is not a distraction from difficulty; it is, however, a healthy coping strategy that helps individuals shift perspective and reconnect with a more hopeful mindset.

Instructions

Introduce the idea that the body and brain respond positively to laughter, often helping to reduce stress, release tension and strengthen feelings of connection with others. Explain that this activity explores how humour and positive moments can lift mood and support emotional regulation, especially during challenging times.

Provide each child with a blank sheet of paper and ask them to draw a tall ladder, labelling it 'The Laugh Ladder'. Explain that the ladder shows how people can move from a low or difficult moment towards feeling lighter and more settled.

- On the bottom rung, children write or draw a situation, feeling or moment that tends to bring their mood down, for example "When I feel left out at breaktime."
- On the middle rungs, they add several examples of things that reliably lift their mood, such as funny memories, people who make them smile, jokes, uplifting films or videos, pets, or small everyday moments of joy.
- On the top rung, they describe how humour or laughter helps them feel, using words such as calmer, lighter, encouraged, connected or hopeful.

Invite children to decorate their ladder with colours, symbols or images that show a sense of rising positivity. When ready, encourage them to share one element that helps them climb from a low moment to a lighter one. Make sharing optional to ensure emotional safety and to respect individual comfort levels.

Discussion Prompts

Use these prompts to help them explore how humour can support emotional balance, connection and resilience.

- How does laughing change how your body feels when you're stressed or upset?
- Who helps you laugh, even on days that feel really hard?
- Can you remember a time when laughing helped you calm down or get on better with someone?
- What's the difference between jokes that make everyone feel included and jokes that make someone feel left out or sad?
- How can little moments of laughing help you handle big feelings?

Extension or Adaptation Options

Use a pre drawn ladder for younger children or those who prefer visual tasks. Older children may extend this into a short reflective piece on how humour helps me cope. In groups, create a shared 'Laugh Ladder' display where contributions can be added anonymously. In one-to-one or alternative provision settings explore comedy clips, songs or stories that support emotion regulation. Families can be encouraged to add to the Laugh Ladder at home to strengthen shared wellbeing practices.

Activity: The Bridge Back

Purpose

This activity supports children to recognise that conflict is a normal part of human connection and that resilience grows when they learn to repair, rather than avoid, relationship challenges. It encourages honest reflection on what damages trust and what helps restore it.

Instructions

Begin by explaining that even strong relationships and friendships can experience tension and that their strength is often shown in how people respond and repair things afterwards. Emphasise that repairing a relationship is a learned skill that supports emotional maturity, empathy and resilience.

Introduce the image of a bridge: just as a bridge links two sides, trust links two people. When something goes wrong, that bridge may feel cracked or broken, but it can be rebuilt with care. Provide each child with a blank sheet of paper and ask them to draw a bridge with a deliberate gap at the centre. They should label one side 'Me' and the other side 'The person I have fallen out with'.

Invite them to write or draw inside the gap what created the break; this might include unkind words, feeling dismissed, misunderstanding someone's intentions or being excluded. Next, ask them to rebuild the bridge by drawing or designing a new connection across the gap. On or around this repaired section, they should add the actions, qualities or conversations that could help mend the relationship. Examples include saying sorry, listening closely, being patient, offering forgiveness or agreeing new boundaries. Allow quiet time for reflection. They can share what they found helpful or hopeful in imagining the repair.

Discussion Prompts

Use these prompts to guide a thoughtful discussion about repairing trust and strengthening relationships after conflict.

- What helps friends make up after an argument?
- How does it feel to say sorry? How does it feel when someone says sorry to you?
- Why can fixing a friendship sometimes make it even stronger?
- What can we learn about ourselves when we work to trust each other again?
- How can these ideas help us get on better with people at the education setting or at home?

Extension or Adaptation Options

Younger children may benefit from bridge templates or emotion picture cards to support expression. Older children could extend the activity through reflective writing or role play exploring apology, empathy and healthy boundaries. In one-to-one or small-group work, the metaphor can support exploration of real experiences in a contained, supported way. As a wider community activity, create a 'Class Bridge' display featuring shared commitments such as 'We listen', 'We take responsibility' and 'We repair' when things go wrong.

Activity: Small Changes, Stronger Me

Purpose

This activity supports children to recognise how the environments and relationships around them influence their mindset, behaviour and resilience. It helps them identify which situations lift them up, which drain their energy and how small, intentional changes can create conditions that support their wellbeing and success.

Instructions

Prepare a whiteboard or flipchart, sticky notes or index cards, pens and a visible rating scale from -2 (unhelpful) to +2 (supportive). Begin with a short discussion about how we are all shaped by the people, routines and places we spend time in. Introduce the idea that resilience does not develop in isolation; it is strengthened by systems that make positive choices easier to maintain. Ask them to identify three places, groups or communities where they spend most of their time. These may include a friendship circle, sports club, online group, classroom or family routine. For each environment, they rate its current impact on their mood, behaviour and effort using the -2 to +2 scale.

Invite them to choose one environment and identify a small, realistic shift they could try over the coming week. This might involve connecting with a more encouraging friend, adjusting the amount of time spent in an online group or changing a daily habit that influences their focus. Record the chosen action on a sticky note to keep visible. After seven days, hold a brief follow-up conversation to explore what they noticed. Highlight even the smallest improvements, reinforcing the message that meaningful change often begins with subtle adjustments.

Discussion Prompts

Use these prompts to help them reflect on how their surroundings influence emotions, behaviour and resilience.

- Which place made you feel the biggest change in your mood or how hard you tried?
- What things around you helped you feel calmer, more motivated or able to concentrate?
- Have you ever seen someone act differently because of the people they were with? What happened?
- What could you do to help someone else feel safe, calm or confident in their space?

Extension or Adaptation Options

For younger children, swap out numbers or written scales for simple visual cues such as coloured dots, emojis or facial-expression cards to help them show how they feel. With older children, encourage them to think about a wider range of environments, including online spaces, friendship groups and community settings. In one-to-one work, link their reflections to personal goals or support plans so they can see how these insights help them make progress. Families can also be invited to explore how home routines, expectations and relationships can strengthen their resilience and emotional wellbeing.

Activity: From Setback to Strength

Purpose

To help children recognise that resilience develops through setbacks, reflection and support. This activity emphasises that challenge is a normal part of growth and that seeking help, adapting plans and maintaining self-belief are essential protective factors in education settings.

Instructions

Begin by introducing the idea that many successful individuals experienced disappointment or criticism long before achieving recognition. Offer a brief, inclusive range of examples: innovators whose ideas were rejected, athletes recovering from injury, campaigners who persisted despite barriers. Show the short YouTube video Famous Failures: Never Give Up to illustrate how early struggles can shape later success. (Available at: https://www.youtube.com/watch?v=5cZh6tYVM2w)

Invite children to choose a well-known figure who faced a meaningful setback. Encourage diversity across gender, culture and field. Ask them to research their chosen person and then create a simple profile or poster using three headings:

- Challenge: the barrier, disappointment or failed attempt.
- Support: people, resources or personal qualities that helped them continue.
- Next Step: how they adapted or moved forward.

Once complete, ask them to share their work in pairs or small groups. Guide them to notice recurring themes such as perseverance, encouragement and the shared human experience of learning through difficulty. Ensure an emotionally safe environment by normalising struggle as part of progress and modelling helpful language such as, "What did you learn from that attempt?"

Discussion Prompts

Use these questions to guide reflection on how setbacks, support and personal strengths work together to build resilience.

- What did you notice or find surprising about the tough moments this person went through?
- How did other people help them keep going or get back on track?
- Which of their ideas, choices or attitudes could help you when things feel hard?
- If you had your own support team who would be in it?
- Can you think of a time when something was challenging but you still learned, improved or felt proud?

Extension or Adaptation Options

Provide illustrated role model cards for younger children so they can easily see and talk about the challenges and strengths of different people. Older children can compare two role models and share what they notice, either in a short presentation or group discussion. In one-to-one sessions or alternative provision, choose a role model from their local community or someone personally meaningful to them, as this can make the learning feel more relevant. To strengthen home-setting links, encourage them to interview a family member about a time they overcame a setback and what helped them keep going.

Connecting the Learning

Supportive relationships do more than help children feel safe and included. They create the emotional conditions in which learning, problem solving and perseverance become possible. When children experience trust, encouragement and belonging, they are more willing to take risks, tolerate uncertainty and remain engaged when things feel difficult. These relationships form a secure base from which challenges can be approached with curiosity rather than fear.

Throughout this unit, children have been supported to identify who and what helps them feel steady, to recognise the qualities of trustworthy relationships and to practise cooperation, repair and mutual support. These experiences strengthen emotional literacy and reinforce the understanding that resilience is not something they must manage alone. Instead, it is built through everyday interactions, where support is both given and received. When education settings consistently model warmth, empathy and relational reliability, children are better equipped to recover from setbacks, seek help appropriately and maintain confidence under pressure.

This relational groundwork is essential. Children who feel supported are more able to think flexibly, manage frustration and persist when solutions are not immediate. As adults, our role is to intentionally design environments where positive connection is predictable and accessible, so that children develop both the networks around them and the confidence within them.

This focus on connection now leads naturally into Unit 11. With a secure relational foundation in place, the next unit explores how children can be taught problem-solving strategies that build on these supportive networks. Together, these units highlight a central message: resilience develops through the interaction between strong relationships and practical skills, each strengthening the other over time.

Unit 11
Teaching Problem-Solving Skills

What this unit covers:

- Learn a problem-solving process, identify, regulate, explore options, act, reflect.
- Build resilience through perseverance, flexible thinking, mistakes, help-seeking, empathy and wise choices.
- Complete practical reflection and creative tasks such as problem-solving scenarios, decision mapping, and resilience-focused discussions.

Introduction

Problem solving sits at the heart of effective learning and healthy development. When children learn how to make sense of a challenge, consider possibilities and move forward with purpose, they are not simply completing a task, they are shaping the way they understand themselves and their capacity to cope in the wider world. This unit examines problem solving as a teachable, practical skill that underpins resilience, wellbeing and academic progress.

Teaching problem solving is not about steering children towards a single correct answer. Instead, it focuses on developing a mindset that notices what is going on, gives time to think and then explores a range of responses or options available. Problem solving is a process, it identifies what the problem actually is, weighs up the options, decides on a course of action and reflects on what has happened. When education settings treat this process as part of everyday learning, children begin to understand that challenges are not signs of failure but invitations to think differently.

Research into nervous system regulation shows that children draw heavily on the emotional cues modelled by the adults around them (Siegel, 2012; Shanker, 2016). When adults demonstrate calm thinking, flexible problem solving and steady decision making under pressure, they provide the nervous system cues that help them feel safe enough to think, explore and try new approaches (Porges, 2011; Siegel, 2012). In this way the behaviour of adults becomes a powerful teaching tool, shaping how children understand challenge and how they learn to respond to it.

DOI: 10.4324/9781003409632-12

The Importance of Problem Solving

Problem solving is one of the most valuable skills we can equip children with. It shapes how they respond to challenge, setback and change, influencing whether they react impulsively or pause, think and act with purpose. Children who develop strong problem-solving skills are more likely to approach difficulties calmly and logically, using strategies rather than giving up when things feel hard. Research consistently identifies problem solving as a key component of emotional wellbeing. D'Zurilla and Nezu (2010) describe it as a coping framework that supports stress management, emotional regulation and sound decision making. In this sense, problem solving is not simply an academic skill, but a foundation for resilience.

Resilience itself is not a fixed personality trait but a learned capacity, built through experience. Each time children work through a problem, they practise managing frustration, regulating emotions and persisting despite difficulty. Over time, this strengthens three core elements of resilience, self-efficacy, the belief that "I can handle this", optimism, the understanding that situations can improve and perseverance, the willingness to keep trying even when progress feels slow. When adults step in too quickly to fix problems, these learning opportunities are reduced. By coaching children through challenges and modelling calm, curious thinking, adults help them build the confidence, creativity and adaptability needed to cope with pressure, recover from mistakes and take ownership of their actions. Education settings that embed problem solving into everyday practice therefore support not only academic progress, but the development of flexible, resilient thinkers.

Practical Ways to Teach Problem Solving

The following activities last between 20 and 40 minutes and are designed for children aged 7 to 14, with adaptations made as needed for younger or older children. Each activity is structured under the following headings, Purpose, Instructions, Discussion Prompts, and Extension or Adaptation. It is important to maintain emotional safety by ensuring that all contributions are respected and valued and by reinforcing that resilience grows through experience and reflection rather than through perfection.

Activity: Brain Teasers

Purpose

This activity offers children a safe, supported opportunity to practise staying with a task when it feels challenging. By engaging with unfamiliar puzzles, they strengthen key resilience skills, sustained effort, emotional regulation, flexible thinking and compassionate self-talk. The aim is to help them recognise that perseverance is a habit they can develop and apply in everyday situations.

Instructions

Begin by explaining that challenge is a normal and valuable part of learning. Share that the puzzles are deliberately tricky, giving them a chance to notice what happens when they meet something that does not make sense straight away. Provide each with an age- appropriate teaser such as a logic grid, pattern challenge, riddle or number puzzle. Encourage experimentation and avoid stepping in too quickly; instead use prompts such as, "What might you try next?" or "Is there another way to look at this?" A visual timer can support pacing without encouraging comparison.

Model calm, steady thinking throughout and normalise emotional responses by saying, "Feeling stuck is part of learning. Let's pause, breathe and choose the next step." Notice and acknowledge effort and strategy use rather than correctness or speed. If frustration builds, offer simple regulation options such as stretching, a drink of water or brief movement, then invite them back when settled. Finish the activity by bringing the group together to reflect on the strategies used and how these might transfer to real-life situations.

Discussion Prompts

Use the following questions to guide reflection and help them make sense of their problem-solving experience.

- What felt challenging and what did you do when you were stuck?
- Which strategies helped you move forward?
- How did it feel to make even a small step of progress?
- Where else could these strategies be useful?
- How can working through something tricky help you become stronger and more confident?

Extension or Adaptation Options

Offer scaffolded puzzles for those who need more support, such as versions with hints, partially completed sections or clearer visual prompts. Provide more complex puzzles for those who are ready for a greater challenge so they can continue stretching their thinking. Link the puzzles to curriculum areas, for example choosing tasks that build mathematical reasoning, pattern recognition or vocabulary skills. Offer take-home puzzles so children can continue practising perseverance and problem solving with family members.

Activity: Learning from Mistakes

Purpose

This activity supports children to recognise mistakes as a natural and useful part of learning. It encourages them to view setbacks as sources of insight, helping them build resilience, confidence and a belief that ability grows through effort.

Instructions

Begin by sharing two or three age-appropriate examples of accidental discoveries, for example penicillin or Post-it Notes. Briefly outline how each discovery began with something going wrong and highlight the attitudes of curiosity, reflection and willingness to try again that helped transform unexpected results into progress. Ask them to think of a personal mistake, a time they misunderstood something, misjudged a situation or took a wrong step and what important lesson they eventually learned from it. Give options for how they record their response, such as a short written note, a sketch or a verbal explanation.

Ask those who wish to share to briefly describe what happened, what they learned and how that learning helped them move forwards. Allow extra time or one-to-one support for those who need it and offer sentence starters if helpful, for example, "At first I thought . . .", "What I realised was . . .".

Discussion Prompts

Use the following prompts to explore how mistakes can lead to learning, innovation and greater resilience:

- What did the inventors do when things went wrong?
- Which attitudes helped them turn an error into something useful?
- How can those same attitudes support us in our setting or daily life?
- How does noticing what we learn from mistakes strengthen resilience?

Extension or Adaptation Options

Offer visual prompts or simplified stories for younger children or those requiring additional support. Older children can research examples from science, art or sport to compare how different fields use trial, error and reflection. Link the activity to literacy, such as short summaries of famous mistakes, PSHE, the importance of resilience and self-regulation or art, through poster designs. For home learning, encourage each to share their useful mistake with family members to spark conversations about persistence and problem solving.

Activity: The 'Ask Three Before Me' Strategy

Purpose

To strengthen independence, constructive help-seeking and collaborative problem solving by guiding children to explore their own ideas and available resources before turning to an adult.

This routine supports resilience by helping them stay with a challenge, think flexibly and use their group as a resource.

Instructions

Introduce 'Ask Three Before Me' as a whole-setting routine that encourages children to pause, think and explore options with increasing confidence. Begin by modelling the sequence clearly:

- Check for yourself. Invite them to reread instructions, revisit what they already know and identify exactly what feels confusing. Demonstrate how slowing down, checking key words or trying a first attempt can reveal solutions.
- Ask one or two friends. Encourage them to approach friends or small groups respectfully, share what they have tried and listen carefully to alternative ideas. Emphasise that peer discussion is not about providing the answer but about helping each other think.
- Use the environment. Guide them to consult books, displays, glossaries, digital tools or any agreed classroom resources. Show how to choose the most reliable source and how to cross check information.

Explain that approaching the adult is the final step used only after all three stages have been attempted with genuine effort. Keep the visual prompt visible and refer to it frequently so the routine becomes embedded. Reinforce the strategy across subjects, celebrating moments when individuals show persistence, thoughtful questioning or effective teamwork.

Discussion Prompts

Use these prompts to reflect on how checking, collaborating and using helpful resources can support learning and resilience.

- What did you discover when you checked your own work first?
- How did asking others help you think differently?
- Which resources were most useful today?
- How does this routine help you stay calm and keep going when something feels difficult?

Extension or Adaptation Options

Use simplified visuals, symbols or scripted prompts to support younger children in understanding each step of the process. For older children, introduce digital reference boards, help seeking checklists or clearly defined peer support roles to encourage independence and collaborative problem solving. Opportunities to practise the approach across different subjects and routines will help embed it as a transferable life skill rather than a one-off strategy.

Activity: The Derek Redmond Story

Purpose

This activity supports children to explore resilience, perseverance, emotional courage and help seeking through a powerful real-life story. Using discussion and a creative completion task, they will consider how determination is shown under pressure and how support from others strengthens coping.

Instructions

Begin by showing the YouTube clip of Derek Redmond's 1992 Olympic 400m race, in which he tears his hamstring but continues the lap with support from his father. Before playing the clip, explain that they will see an example of someone facing an unexpected setback and making a choice about how to respond. After watching, allow a short moment of quiet reflection and lead a supportive dialogue using the discussion prompts below.

Introduce the creative task, 'I've Started, So I'll Finish'. Give each an incomplete image or pattern, such as half-drawn shapes or an unfinished scene. Explain that their job is to complete it in their own way. Emphasise that there is no single correct outcome; the focus is on continuing, adapting and making meaning from what is already there. As they work, move around the group, noticing effort, encouraging problem solving and modelling supportive language. When everyone has finished invite the children to share their designs and talk about any moments when they had to keep going despite uncertainty. Link their creative choices back to resilience.

Discussion Prompts

Use these prompts to help them reflect on Derek's story and explore what determination, perseverance and seeking support can look like in real life.

- What did you notice about Derek's determination?
- Why might someone continue when something becomes difficult or painful?
- What does this story show about the courage required to ask for help?
- How did it feel to complete something that began unfinished?
- Can you recall a time you wanted to give up but continued?
- How might perseverance or support help with your education or life challenges?

Extension Options

Older children can write a short reflective piece linking Derek's experience to a challenge they have faced themselves, with a focus on perseverance, coping strategies and the role of support from others. This may be guided with prompt questions or sentence starters to deepen thinking. Younger groups can work with simplified images, discussion cards or a brief, teacher-led role play that explores themes of keeping going, trying again or asking for help when things feel difficult. As a group, they may collaboratively create one large unfinished artwork that everyone contributes to, reinforcing ideas of teamwork, shared effort and collective resilience.

Activity: See It, Own It, Change It

Purpose

This activity helps children build resilience by developing self-awareness and personal responsibility. Through relatable scenarios, they learn to notice thoughts and feelings, understand how their actions affect others and explore constructive choices that support emotional regulation and healthier relationships.

Instructions

Introduce one or more short age-appropriate scenarios that reflect common social or emotional challenges, for example, "A friend shared something you asked them to keep private", "You were blamed for something you did not do" or "You felt left out when others made plans without you." Present scenarios as cards, slides or simple verbal descriptions. Ask them to work individually or in small groups and explore the situation using three reflective steps.

See It: "What is happening here?" Encourage clear description of the situation, including feelings, thoughts and assumptions.

Own It: "What part did I play?" Support them to consider their contribution through choices, reactions or communication, emphasising that responsibility is not the same as blame.

Change It: "What could I do next time?" Encourage them to identify practical, prosocial alternatives that could help them respond more effectively in future situations.

Invite everyone to note, draw their reflections or share them verbally. Reinforce that this is a safe space for exploring ideas, not finding a right answer.

Discussion Prompts

Use these questions to help them deepen their understanding of the scenario and explore different perspectives and choices.

- What helped you understand what was really going on?
- What different choices did you notice you could make?
- How do you think the other person might have felt in that moment?

Extension or Adaptation Options

Younger children may use visuals, puppets or simple, adult-led role play to explore the scenarios in an accessible, low-pressure way. Older children can apply the steps to real situations from education setting or home through discussion or short reflection activities to build everyday problem-solving skills. The activity links well with PSHE, literacy, art or science through storytelling, drawing or exploring cause-and-effect. Families can also use the three steps at home to support calmer, more constructive conversations and consistent responses.

Activity: The '5 Whys' Technique to Build Resilience

Purpose

This activity supports children to strengthen emotional regulation and problem solving by looking beneath the surface of behaviour. Through structured, curious questioning, they learn to pause, reflect and recognise the emotions or unmet needs driving a reaction. This helps them respond with greater empathy, clarity and resilience in education settings and beyond.

Instructions

Begin by introducing the '5 Whys' as a simple thinking tool designed to uncover what is really going on beneath a behaviour or emotional response. Explain that the aim is understanding and not blame. Guide them through the following five steps:

1. Describe the situation clearly.
2. Ask "Why?"
3. Use the answer to form the next "Why?"
4. Continue until a root cause begins to appear.
5. Consider a constructive, calm next step.

Model the process using a familiar scenario, such as "A child swears at you." Guide the group through each of the '5 Whys', demonstrating how initial reactions often hide deeper feelings such as embarrassment, overwhelm or a sense of unfairness. Think aloud during the process, modelling how curiosity can reduce tension. Next place them in pairs or small groups, give each group a new scenario to explore, for example "Someone refuses to join in", "Someone storms off" or "Someone says it's boring." Ask them to record each question, answer and insight, focusing on what might sit underneath the behaviour and how that understanding could shape a more helpful response.

Discussion Prompts

Use these prompts to explore how understanding the deeper causes of behaviour can shape calmer more effective responses.

- When you looked again, did it help you see what happened in a new way?
- If we understand why someone acted that way, what might we try next time?
- How does it feel when someone really listens to you? Does it help you feel calmer or fix the problem?
- How did your voice and your body help when you asked your question?

Extension or Adaptation Options

Adapt the number of 'Whys' to suit children's confidence and developmental level. Younger children may benefit from a simple visual 'Why Ladder' to help them follow the thinking step by step, while older children can extend the task through role play, short written reflections or by linking the approach to PSHE, literacy or art activities. Families can also be encouraged to use a simplified ladder at home to support calm, curiosity-driven conversations and shared problem solving.

Activity: The Story Behind the Snapshot

Purpose

This activity strengthens empathy, flexible thinking and perspective taking by helping children recognise that a single moment never tells the whole story. By exploring multiple interpretations of everyday situations, they learn to pause, question their assumptions and approach others with curiosity and compassion, an essential foundation of resilience in education settings.

Instructions

Prepare a selection of ambiguous photographs or short written scenarios. These should depict everyday moments that could be interpreted in several ways, for example a child sitting alone, a group whispering, someone appearing frustrated or a friend who has not replied to a message. Present one photograph or scenario at a time. Ask the group: "What do you think is happening here?" Invite as many interpretations as possible and reassure them that there is no single correct answer. Encourage descriptive thinking, for example, "What makes you say that?" and support individuals who may need additional prompts or visual cues. After gathering a range of ideas, share the actual context behind the photograph or scenario. Guide them to reflect on how their initial assumptions changed once more information became available. Repeat with several examples, gradually increasing difficulty. Emphasise that slowing down our thinking helps us respond more thoughtfully during real life social interactions.

Discussion Prompts

Use these prompts to explore how our first impressions can change when we pause, look deeper and consider different perspectives.

- What influenced your first interpretation?
- What else might have been happening?
- How did your thinking shift when you learned the true context?
- How could pausing before reacting help us manage tricky situations?
- How might understanding different perspectives support stronger relationships?

Extension or Adaptation Options

Use picture books or simple illustrations with younger children to support discussion and shared interpretation. Older children can be invited to create their own ambiguous images or short narratives for others to explore and interpret, encouraging deeper thinking and empathy. The activity links well with PSHE, literacy, art or science by examining how perspective, evidence and inference shape understanding. Children may also take an image home to discuss with family members or use this technique independently to reflect on times when assumptions have influenced their thoughts, feelings or reactions.

Activity: Choose Your Own Way

Purpose

This activity supports children to strengthen self-regulation and thoughtful decision making. By pausing to notice needs, consider consequences and choose actions with care, each can build personal responsibility, emotional control and resilience in everyday situations.

Instructions

Create or display a large compass with four points, labelled 'N - Needs', 'E - Effects', 'S - Solutions' and 'W - Wise Choice'. Explain that this compass offers a calm, structured way to navigate strong emotions or tricky moments, introduce each point clearly:

- Needs: "What do I need right now to feel settled or understood?"
- Effects: "What might happen if I act on this feeling?"
- Solutions: "What options do I have?"
- Wise Choice: "Which option feels fair, respectful and likely to lead to a positive outcome?"

Model the process using an everyday scenario, such as feeling annoyed when someone interrupts or wanting to give up on a challenging task. Speak your thoughts aloud so they can hear how to move step-by-step through the compass. Invite children to apply the compass to a current or recent challenge. They can talk it through with you, sketch their responses or jot brief notes. Support them to slow the moment down, explore possibilities and notice the difference between reacting and responding.

Discussion Prompts

Use these prompts to explore how noticing our needs and choices can help us stay calm, make wise decisions and feel more in control.

- When you stop for a moment, does it help you notice what you really need?
- How can thinking before we act help us feel more in charge of what happens next?
- What does making a good choice feel like in your body or in your mind?
- How could using the compass help you feel braver or calmer when your feelings are big?

Extension or Adaptation Options

Use visuals, picture cues or simplified wording to support younger children or those who find emotional vocabulary challenging. Older children can apply the compass to more complex situations such as peer relationships, online behaviour or academic pressures. Children may also take the compass home to support family conversations and personal reflection beyond their education setting.

Activity: The Decision Domino

Purpose

This activity supports children to recognise how everyday choices shape their experiences, confidence and resilience. By breaking down a single decision into its key stages, they can notice patterns, understand consequences and develop a more thoughtful approach to future actions. The emphasis is on learning not judging.

Instructions

Provide each with a strip of paper or template divided into three clear sections, 'My Choice', 'What Happened', and 'What I Learned'. Invite them to think of a recent decision big or small made within their setting or in daily life and encourage them to record brief notes or symbols in each section. Once completed, pair individuals or create small groups. Ask them to talk through their decision with a friend, focusing on what they discovered about how they make choices. Remind the group that the purpose is reflection not comparison. Guide them to explore what influenced their choice, how the outcome felt and what they might take forward into future situations. Offer neutral examples for anyone who finds it difficult to identify a situation, such as choosing how to respond to a disagreement or deciding how to spend breaktime. Maintain a supportive tone and reinforce that every decision offers an opportunity for growth.

Discussion Prompts

Use these questions to help you think about the choice you made and what you learned from it.

- What did you notice about how you made your choice?
- Did anything or anyone help you decide?
- If the same thing happened again would you do anything differently?
- What does this choice show about what you're good at?
- What did this experience teach you about keeping going when things are tough?

Extension or Adaptation Options

Use drawings or simple visual cues with younger children to help them show the choices they made and what happened next. For older children, extend the activity by exploring how emotions, pressure or expectations may have influenced their decisions and outcomes. Create a 'Decision Domino Wall' using anonymised examples to display learning, helping the group recognise shared experiences and normalise thoughtful reflection.

Activity: Flip the Problem

Purpose

This activity helps children build resilience by learning how to reframe limiting thoughts into purposeful, solution focused questions. By practising this shift, they start to view challenges as issues to investigate rather than barriers that shape their identity. The aim is to strengthen confidence, flexible thinking and the belief that progress is possible with effort and curiosity.

Instructions

Introduce the idea that the words we use especially in moments of difficulty shape how we respond. Share a simple example such as "I'll never get this right." Then model how to turn it into a constructive question: "What could I try differently?" or "Who might help me understand this?" Invite children to think of a recent challenge and write down a statement that reflects their initial reaction. Ask them to flip the statement by turning it into a question beginning with 'How?', 'What?' or 'Who?'. Next support them to generate a wide range of possible ways forward, aiming for at least ten ideas, encouraging creativity and reminding them that even small or seemingly unrealistic ideas can spark useful thinking. Finally guide them to choose one or two practical actions they can test over the coming week. Encourage them to record these choices somewhere visible so they can review their progress.

Discussion Prompts

Use these questions to emphasise that reframing is not about ignoring difficulties but about opening up possibilities.

- How did it feel when you changed your stuck thought into a question?
- Which idea do you think you could try first?
- How might things change if you tried thinking about future challenges in this way?

Extension or Adaptation Options

Use visual prompts or simple sentence starters to support younger children in understanding and practising reframing. Older children can apply reframing to academic goals, friendships or wellbeing themes, including through reflective journals or discussion. This approach works well across PSHE, literacy and pastoral interventions and can be shared with families to reinforce resilient thinking beyond the setting.

Activity: The Paper Tower Challenge

Purpose

This activity strengthens resilience by inviting children to adapt, problem solve and collaborate when circumstances shift unexpectedly. Through practical experimentation, they learn that plans may not always go as expected but flexible thinking, communication and persistence help them move forward.

Instructions

Begin by placing children into small teams. Explain that their task is to build the tallest free-standing tower they can using only a set number of paper sheets, for example ten to fifteen. Clarify the rules: no tape, glue or additional resources and the structure must stand independently without leaning on any surface. Set a clear time limit of five to ten minutes and encourage teams to explore different design ideas, such as rolled columns, folded supports, triangular bases, and to talk through what makes some structures stronger or more stable. When time is up, measure the towers and guide a brief reflection on what supported success and what challenges arose.

Next, introduce a new constraint to build resilience under changing conditions. Options include reducing the number of sheets, shortening the time, placing the tower on an uneven surface or asking it to hold a small object. Invite teams to rebuild or adapt their original design in response to the new rule. After the second attempt, ask each group to share what they changed, how they managed setbacks and what they noticed about communication, flexibility and persistence. Finish by linking the activity to real-life situations where plans shift and individuals must adjust their approach.

Discussion Prompts

Use these prompts to think about how being flexible and working together can help us handle challenges.

- How did you feel when your first idea didn't work?
- What helped your team adapt when the rules changed?
- Which strategies supported effective communication?
- How might flexibility help in everyday challenges?

Extension or Adaptation Options

Offer extra time, simplified rules or a limited amount of tape to support younger children in accessing the activity. Increase the level of challenge for older children by adding weight-bearing elements or introducing mid-task changes that require them to adapt their plan. This activity links well with science, design and technology, PE and PSHE and can also be repeated at home to encourage reflection on problem solving and adapting when plans change.

Activity: Coaching Through Challenge

Purpose

This activity aims to strengthen resilience by modelling language that helps children interpret difficulty as part of the learning journey. When adults use supportive, growth-focused prompts, children are more likely to persist, reflect and recognise that progress comes through effort and practice. Over time, this approach helps to build a culture where curiosity, perseverance and emotional regulation are valued.

Instructions

Introduce the idea of coaching through challenge as a daily communication habit rather than a one-off technique. Explain that the language adults use during moments of frustration or uncertainty can either increase resilience or limit it. Share a set of purposeful resilience prompts such as:

- "What could you try differently?"
- "You're not there yet what might help you get closer?"

- "That didn't go to plan and what have you learned from it?"
- "What's your plan B?"
- "I can see you're sticking with this - your persistence is making a difference."
- "Let's look at this mistake as information, not failure."

Model how and when to use these prompts during academic tasks, social dilemmas or emotional challenges. Emphasise the importance of tone - calm, curious and genuinely supportive. Encourage them to pause before offering solutions so they can think through possibilities themselves. Reinforce that consistency matters: the more adults use reflective, growth-oriented language, the more confidently children internalise these patterns as tools for managing setbacks.

Discussion Prompts

Use these prompts to explore how encouraging words and recognising effort can help us stay motivated and find solutions when things feel tough.

- How does it feel when someone notices your effort rather than the outcome?
- Which types of language help you keep going when something is hard?
- How do these prompts help you shift from feeling stuck to exploring solutions?

Extension or Adaptation Options

Use visual cues, sentence starters or simple role play to help younger children practise supportive and resilient language. Older children can extend the activity by creating their own resilience phrases or encouragements to support friends in different situations. This approach links well with PSHE, literacy, creative subjects and physical education and families can be encouraged to use similar language at home to help build confidence and resilience over time.

Connecting the Learning

Teaching problem solving is more than helping children get through a single difficult moment; it is about shaping how they interpret challenge, how they speak to themselves under pressure and how confidently they believe they can influence what happens next. Across this unit, children have practised the habits that sit at the heart of effective problem solving, noticing what is happening, managing emotional responses, exploring different perspectives, seeking support when needed, generating options and reflecting on outcomes. Over time, these habits begin to form a resilient internal narrative, "I can pause", "I can think", "I can try another way."

When adults model calm curiosity, resist the urge to fix problems too quickly and create space for reflection, they protect the learning process itself. Children learn that difficulty is not a signal to stop, but a prompt to think differently. Mistakes become information, effort becomes meaningful and perseverance becomes a skill rather than a personality trait. In environments where effort, curiosity and learning from experience are consistently valued, children begin to see themselves as capable problem solvers who can cope, adapt and recover.

This shift in thinking creates a natural bridge to the next stage of learning. While this unit has focused on navigating challenges as they arise, Unit 12 builds on these foundations by exploring how problem-solving skills can be applied over time through structured goal setting. Moving from responding to immediate difficulties to shaping longer term aims helps children translate resilience into direction. They begin to see that the same skills used to work through a problem can also help them plan, persevere and make progress towards goals that matter to them. By connecting problem solving with purposeful goal setting, children are supported not only to manage challenges, but to take increasing ownership of their learning, behaviour and personal growth. In doing so, they move from coping with what is in front of them to actively shaping what comes next.

Unit 12
Teaching Goal Setting for Motivation and Persistence

What this unit covers:

- Understand how clear, achievable goals build motivation, persistence, self-regulation and confidence.
- Use the GROW model to help children set goals, review reality, explore options and plan next steps.
- Complete practical reflection and creative tasks such as purpose-mapping, mission ladders and commitment calendars.

Introduction

Helping children set purposeful, manageable goals is central to strengthening resilience. When approached with clarity and care, goal setting offers more than a roadmap for learning it provides a disciplined structure through which they can understand where they are, where they want to be and how they might get there. This process gives direction and supports sustained effort without overwhelming them. It becomes a practical means through which focus, motivation and emotional steadiness can grow.

Drawing on established educational and psychological research, this unit examines how carefully framed goals contribute to the development of perseverance, reflective thinking and a sense of self-efficacy. When children see that their actions lead to progress, however small, they begin to recognise their own capacity to influence outcomes. The unit also introduces structured approaches, including the GROW Model, to support practitioners in guiding children from initial intention to purposeful action. Therefore, goal setting is positioned as a steady, supportive process through which they experience progress, confidence and long-term personal development.

The Importance of Goal Setting

Goal setting is far more than a motivational exercise; it is a developmental process that shapes identity, self-belief and resilience. When children learn to define, pursue and reflect

DOI: 10.4324/9781003409632-13

on meaningful goals, they develop essential psychological tools for learning, commitment and optimism. Central to this process is self-efficacy, defined by Bandura (1997) as the belief in one's ability to influence outcomes. Through setting and achieving manageable goals, children strengthen this belief, which in turn promotes persistence, emotional regulation and sustained engagement with challenge. Locke and Latham's (2002) goal setting theory further demonstrates that specific, appropriately challenging goals, supported by constructive feedback, lead to higher levels of motivation and performance.

Goal setting also plays a critical role in the development of executive functioning and self-regulation. As children learn to plan, prioritise and delay gratification, they build the capacity to resist short-term rewards in favour of long-term purpose (Mischel et al., 1989). These skills underpin self control and resilience, enabling children to manage frustration, maintain focus and sustain effort over time. When children experience that their actions make a difference, they begin to internalise the belief that effort leads to progress, a core principle of a growth mindset (Dweck, 2006).

Resilience develops through repeated experiences of persistence, reflection and recovery after difficulty. Goal setting strengthens each of these processes by providing a structured framework through which children can practise overcoming obstacles and recognising progress. Through structured goal setting experiences, children develop self-regulation by managing impulses and maintaining focus despite setbacks, persistence by sustaining effort when results are not immediate, optimism by viewing setbacks as temporary rather than permanent failures and agency by recognising that their choices and actions influence outcomes. Research into resilience consistently highlights the importance of perceived control and problem-solving skills in coping with adversity (Masten, 2014; American Psychological Association, 2020). When children set their own goals and monitor their progress, they learn that success is not a matter of luck but the result of deliberate and sustained action. This understanding fosters a sense of internal stability, confidence and adaptability when navigating uncertainty.

Using the GROW Model for Goal Setting

The GROW model provides a clear, structured process that helps children turn aspirations into achievement through four stages, which include the 'Goal', 'Reality', 'Options' and 'Way Forward'. Developed by Whitmore (1992) for leadership coaching it is now widely used in education. In classrooms, the GROW model promotes planning, perseverance and adaptability, key skills for resilience, guiding them to reflect, problem solve and take ownership of their progress.

The model can be embedded across the curriculum, including in PSHE, mentoring and subject-based reflection. Research shows that structured coaching approaches such as GROW can also improve education settings' attendance by enhancing motivation, goal clarity and self-regulation (Passmore, van Nieuwerburgh and Barr, 2019). For example, a child might set the 'Goal', "I want to speak more confidently in class discussions", recognise the 'Reality', "I often know the answer but hesitate to share it", explore 'Options' like "I could practise with a friend or prepare one answer in advance" and define a 'Way Forward', "This week I'll prepare one idea before each class and speak at least once per day." This simple structure builds ownership, persistence and reflective learning skills that extend far beyond the classroom.

Practical Ways to Teach Goal Setting

The following activities last between 20 and 40 minutes and are designed for children aged 7 to 14, with adaptations made as needed for younger or older children. Each activity is structured under the following headings, Purpose, Instructions, Discussion Prompts, and Extension or Adaptation. It is important to maintain emotional safety by ensuring that all contributions are respected and valued and by reinforcing that resilience grows through experience and reflection rather than through perfection.

Activity: The Purpose Behind the Goal

Purpose

This activity supports children to look beyond the surface of a goal and reconnect with the deeper purpose that makes it meaningful to them. When they understand why a goal matters, they are more able to sustain motivation, manage frustration and maintain resilience during periods of challenge or slow progress.

Instructions

Begin by acknowledging that motivation naturally rises and falls, particularly when a goal requires ongoing effort. Explain that returning to the purpose behind a goal can help reignite energy, direction and emotional steadiness. Ask them to choose one personal goal and reflect on two questions:

- Why does this goal matter to me?
- How might achieving it make a difference to my life or to others?

Provide a range of ways to capture their thinking, such as a written reflection, a mind map or a symbolic drawing. Encourage them to personalise their work with colours, images or words that act as visual prompts to their purpose. Allow reflection time before inviting sharing in pairs or small groups. Emphasise that the focus is on understanding themselves, not judging the quality of the goal or comparing progress. Remind them that fluctuating motivation is normal and that reconnecting with purpose is a practical tool for self-regulation and persistence.

Discussion Prompts

Use the questions below to explore their motivation and deepen their understanding of what drives them to keep moving toward their goal.

- Why is your goal important to you? What makes it matter?
- When things get tough, how can thinking about your reason for doing this help you keep going?
- What could you do to help yourself remember your goal and why it's important?
- How could talking about your goal with someone you trust help you stick with it?

Extension or Adaptation Options

Younger children may prefer to express their sense of purpose through drawing or collage. Older children could create a purpose map, visually linking a personal goal to their values, strengths, supportive people and practical next steps. In one-to-one or pastoral sessions, this activity can be used to explore how having a clear sense of purpose supports emotional regulation and decision making. Families can be invited to create and share purpose cards at home, where a child writes or draws something that matters to them and why, to encourage ongoing conversations about motivation, resilience and perseverance.

Activity: The Mission Ladder

Purpose

The 'Mission Ladder' supports children to strengthen resilience by setting a meaningful short- term goal and breaking it into small, achievable actions. By visualising progress and anticipating challenges, they practise planning, perseverance, emotional regulation and adaptive thinking, which are core components of resilience.

Instructions

Introduce a mission as a personal goal that feels important, realistic and achievable within a short timeframe. Emphasise that missions do not need to be dramatic small intentions often build the strongest habits. Invite children to reflect on a goal they care about by using prompts such as "What would you like to make progress on this week?" "What feels important to you right now?" Allow brief discussion to help them connect with their idea.

Provide each with a simple ladder template containing five or six rungs. Ask them to write their mission at the top of the ladder, explaining that each rung represents one small step towards achieving it. Support them to break the mission into three to five manageable steps, ensuring each step is specific and realistic. Encourage them to think about potential barriers, such as confidence, time-demands or resources and to note strategies for managing these, including practising at regular times, asking for support or using positive self-talk.

Once complete, invite them to colour, tick or decorate each rung as they progress. Plan regular check-ins so they can review their ladder, notice patterns and adjust steps where needed. Encourage them to share their mission with a trusted adult or friend who can offer encouragement and accountability.

Discussion Prompts

Use the following prompts to support a reflective discussion that helps them clarify what motivates them and recognise the strategies that sustain progress.

- What part of your mission feels most motivating?
- How will you recognise progress?
- What might help you stay focused when things feel difficult?
- If you feel stuck, what could you try next?
- What have you discovered about yourself so far?

Extension or Adaptation Options

Use drawings or symbols for younger children, keeping missions to two or three steps. Older children can develop a mission reflection journal or digital tracker. In one-to-one sessions, link each rung to strengths and emotional regulation strategies. In groups, use peer-sharing and check-ins to build motivation. Families can create shared ladders to strengthen home-setting connection.

Activity: Do One Thing Today

Purpose

This activity helps children understand that resilience grows through steady, manageable actions. By committing to one realistic step each day, they build confidence, self-regulation and a sense of personal agency, all key protective factors in education settings.

Instructions

Begin by explaining that meaningful progress rarely comes from sudden bursts of effort. Instead, achievements in learning, wellbeing and relationships typically develop through regular, repeated actions. Share examples, such as practising a skill, asking for help or taking a moment to calm the body before responding. Invite each to identify a goal connected to something they want to strengthen, for example confidence, focus or friendships. Once they have chosen, guide them through three reflective questions:

- What is one small thing you could do today that moves you a step closer?
- How might you feel after completing it?
- What could get in the way and how will you manage that?

Encourage them to record their responses in a journal, goal card or digital note. Explain that writing things down helps make intentions clearer and easier to follow through. Ask them to keep their chosen action somewhere visible so they can revisit it regularly. Invite them to review their action each day or week, paying attention to any patterns they notice moments when the task felt easier, times when they avoided it or situations that helped them succeed. Support them to reflect on what helped, what got in the way and what they might try differently next time.

Discussion Prompts

These prompts can support a thoughtful discussion that highlights how steady, manageable actions contribute to personal growth and sustained resilience.

- What helps you take small steps even when motivation dips?
- How does making steady progress affect your confidence?
- Can you recall a time when small actions led to something meaningful?
- What have you learned about yourself through this process?
- How do setbacks help you rethink your next small step?

Extension or Adaptation Options

Use visual supports such as sticker paths or simple progress charts with younger children to help them see their effort building over time. Older children may enjoy turning this into a short, time-limited challenge, for example 21 days of daily actions, where they track one small, consistent behaviour linked to a wider goal. In one-to-one work, link the activity directly to personal targets or behaviour plans to reinforce accountability and reflection. Families can also be involved by choosing their own one small step to work on, modelling consistency and positive habit-building at home.

Activity: The Commitment Calendar

Purpose

The 'Commitment Calendar' supports children to recognise that resilience is strengthened through steady, manageable actions. By tracking small daily commitments, they experience a sense of ownership over their progress and begin to understand that meaningful change grows from consistency rather than intensity.

Instructions

Begin by acknowledging that long-term goals can feel overwhelming, whereas breaking them into small, repeatable actions makes progress possible. Invite those taking part to choose a goal that matters to them; this may relate to a personal skill, wellbeing habit or a specific area of learning. Ask them to identify one simple action they can commit to each day. Encourage steps that are realistic and achievable, for example practising a hobby for ten minutes, completing a short organising task or intentionally offering kindness. Guide them through a short reflection before they begin:

- What small action will support your goal each day?
- How will you remind yourself to follow through?
- What helpful phrase can you use when motivation drops?
- How will you notice and celebrate progress?

Provide each with a calendar grid and each day they complete their chosen action, they mark, colour or place a symbol in the box. Emphasise that this visual record is designed to show effort over time, not perfection. Review the calendars at the end of each week or month. Explore what helped them stay on track, where they struggled and how their confidence has developed. Reinforce that resilience grows when they return to their goal after setbacks.

Discussion Prompts

The following prompts can help deepen reflection on the experiences, challenges and personal insights that emerged as progress accumulated over time.

- How did it feel to see your progress building over time?
- What supported you on days when you found it difficult?
- What did you notice about your habits or motivation?
- When you nearly gave up, what helped you continue?
- How might these insights help in another area of your life?

Extension or Adaptation Options

Use symbols, stickers or other simple visual prompts with younger children to support understanding and engagement. Older children may benefit from adding a brief reflective journal alongside the activity to record thoughts, feelings, successes and challenges as they go. In group settings, they can create a shared calendar linked to a collective goal, such as cooperation, kindness or mutual respect, with progress reviewed together. In therapeutic or alternative provision settings, the timeframe can be shortened to help maintain focus and motivation. Families can also use a simplified home version of the activity to encourage shared responsibility, positive routines and the celebration of progress.

Activity: Dealing with Obstacles

Purpose

This activity supports children to view obstacles as a predictable and manageable part of working towards any goal. It encourages them to build resilience by anticipating challenges, practising emotional regulation and developing practical strategies they can use when things feel difficult.

Instructions

Begin by explaining that every meaningful goal involves moments that test motivation, confidence or patience. Reassure them that encountering difficulties is not a sign that they are doing something wrong; it is simply part of progress. Ask each to choose a realistic goal they are currently working towards. This might relate to friendships, learning a new skill, managing a feeling or completing a personal project. Provide paper or a structured goal- planning sheet. Guide them carefully through the following steps:

- Invite them to name their chosen goal clearly.
- Ask "What might get in the way?", supporting them to think about emotional, practical or personal obstacles.
- For each obstacle ask "If this happens, what could I try?", "Who could support me?" and "What could I say to myself to stay steady?"
- Encourage them to write brief action steps or coping strategies for each identified challenge.
- Remind them that planning ahead increases confidence and makes it easier to stay on track when difficulties arise.

Discussion Prompts

Use these questions to help them think about what helps them get ready for challenges and keep going when things feel tricky.

- How did it feel to think about things that might be hard before they happen?
- What kinds of things can you say to yourself to help you stay calm or keep trying?
- How could asking someone for help make your goal easier to stick to?
- Can you remember a time when you didn't give up and things worked out in the end?

Extension or Adaptation Options

For younger children, simplify the challenge by focusing on a single, everyday obstacle; for example, frame the task as "What can I do if this feels too hard?" and encourage them to use drawings, puppets or simple role-play scenarios to rehearse possible responses. For older children, extend the task into a more detailed resilience route map, where a central goal branches into different roads, representing strategies, decision points and sources of support for various challenges. In one-to-one or home environments, involve parents by inviting them to talk through anticipated obstacles with the child and co-create simple, supportive plans.

Activity: The Brave Step Challenge

Purpose

Resilience grows when children experience themselves coping with uncertainty and stretching their comfort zones safely. The 'Brave Step Challenge' helps them identify a goal they feel unsure about and practise taking a small, intentional step towards it. This builds a sense of agency, strengthens emotional regulation and reinforces the belief that courage is something they develop through action.

Instructions

Invite children to quietly reflect on something they would like to try but currently feel hesitant or nervous about. This could be speaking up in class, joining a new activity, or asking for help when they need it. Reassure them that this is a private and personal choice, and that everyone's goal will be different.

Give each child a small card and ask them to write their chosen goal at the top. Support them to think through the following reflective questions:

- What is the smallest, most manageable step you could take to begin?
- Who could support or encourage you when you give it a try?
- How would you like to feel once you have taken this step?

Create a visible courage wall in the room and invite children to place their cards on it as a commitment to themselves. When a child completes their chosen step, invite them to move their card to the 'I Did It!' section. Acknowledge each child's effort discreetly and positively, ensuring the environment remains supportive, safe and focused on personal progress rather than comparison or competition.

Discussion Prompts

Use the following prompts to guide a reflective conversation that help them recognise the small but significant shifts they made during the activity.

- How did it feel to take your first brave step?
- What helped you move forward even if/when you felt unsure?
- What did you learn about your courage or confidence?
- How did seeing your goal on the courage wall effect your motivation?

Extension or Adaptation Options

Use images, symbols or simple sentence starters to support younger children in identifying and naming acts of courage. For older children, extend the activity by linking their examples to wider personal goals, character development or emerging leadership responsibilities. Revisit the courage wall regularly to notice patterns of growth, celebrate progress and prompt reflective discussion. For those who prefer personal or private reflection, offer an individual courage journal as an alternative or additional option.

Activity: Changing the Voice in Your Head

Purpose

This activity supports children to notice the impact of their inner voice on confidence, effort and perseverance. By learning to replace unhelpful self-talk with more supportive alternatives, they build emotional regulation and enhance their capacity to stay focused on goals, even when progress feels slow or challenging.

Instructions

Before the session, prepare a flipchart or whiteboard with two headings, 'Unhelpful Self Talk' and 'Helpful Self-Talk'. Add a few example statements under each heading to prompt discussion. If available, create simple self-talk swap cards showing contrasting phrases, and arrange the room so children can work in pairs or small groups.

Begin by explaining that self-talk disd the inner voice or commentary we all have, especially when something feels challenging. Explain that this inner voice can influence how we feel, how we behave and whether we keep trying or give up. Normalise the experience by reminding the group that everyone experiences self-doubt at times.

Invite them to read the statements on the board and decide which column they belong in. As you discuss the answers, encourage children to reflect on how unhelpful and helpful self-talk might affect their emotions, behaviour and motivation. Make the link to resilience by highlighting how supportive self-talk helps us stay calmer, more regulated and focused on solutions.

Next, model how to reframe unhelpful self-talk. For example, show how "I can't do this" can become "I can't do this yet" or "I can try a different strategy." Ask children to practise reframing in pairs, using the swap cards or by generating examples from their own experiences in school, sport or friendships. To finish, ask each child to choose a goal that matters to them and write down two helpful self-talk statements they could use when they feel frustrated or stuck. Encourage them to visualise using these statements during future challenges, reinforcing the idea that what we say to ourselves can support persistence and confidence.

Discussion Prompts

These prompts can guide a reflective conversation that helps them explore how their inner dialogue shapes their responses to challenge and the choices they make.

- How does the way you talk to yourself change what you do when something feels hard?
- Can you think of a time when saying something kind or helpful to yourself helped you keep going?
- What do you think would happen if we always believed the unhelpful thoughts in our heads?
- How could helpful self-talk help you in other parts of your life, like with friends, at home or in sport?
- How can we help each other notice unhelpful self-talk and change it into something more helpful?

Extension or Adaptation Options

Use storytelling, drawings, role play or puppets with younger children to help them explore feelings in an engaging way. With older children, deepen the activity by linking it to performance psychology, exam preparation or strategies for managing pressure. For children with additional needs, provide simplified language, a reduced cognitive load and clear visual supports. This activity also works effectively in one-to-one pastoral support, targeted interventions, or family-based work, where a higher level of trust and personalised reflection can be developed and ideas can be revisited over time.

Activity: The Mountain of Me

Purpose

To help children recognise how effort, setbacks and support shape personal growth. This activity strengthens self-awareness, confidence and ownership by encouraging children to explore a challenge they worked hard to overcome.

Instructions

Invite them to draw a large outline of a mountain and title it 'The Mountain of Me'. Explain that the mountain represents a real challenge they have faced or are currently facing. It should be something that required determination, patience and courage. Throughout the activity, model calm reflection and reinforce the message that every mountain is different and everyone's journey looks unique.

- At the base of the mountain, ask them to write one specific challenge, such as learning a new skill, managing anxiety in social situations or trying something unfamiliar.
- Along the sides of the mountain, guide them to record moments when the challenge felt hard. Encourage honesty by exploring times when motivation dropped, frustration appeared or they doubted whether they could continue.
- Next, ask them to add what helped them keep going. This might include support from others, a helpful strategy, a change in mindset or taking the challenge one small step at a time.
- At the summit, invite them to describe what progress looked and felt like. Emphasise that reaching the top does not mean the challenge is completely solved or done perfectly. The summit represents growth, such as feeling braver, stronger, more confident or more capable than before.

Discussion Prompts

These prompts can help guide a reflective conversation about the personal challenges, turning-points and moments of strength that emerged throughout the activity.

- What made this challenge hard for you?
- When did you feel like giving up and what helped you keep going?

- How did your feelings or confidence change as you progressed?
- What does your summit represent, for example progress, courage or something else?
- How might these understandings help you with future challenges?

Extension or Adaptation Options

Use simple templates, sentence starters or verbal scaffolding to support younger children in identifying their strengths and strategies. Encourage older children to add a written reflection explaining how the strategies they used on their mountain could support future resilience or be applied to new challenges. In group settings, combine individual mountains to create a shared 'Mountain Range of Us' display that celebrates collective strengths. Invite families to create their own mountains at home to reinforce shared language and encourage positive conversations beyond the session.

Activity: Celebrating the Steps

Purpose

This activity helps children recognise the value of sustained effort, small improvements and the everyday actions that build resilience. By shifting attention from end results to the process of learning, they begin to understand that progress is made through steady, purposeful steps.

Instructions

Begin by inviting the group to reflect on how success is usually noticed in their education setting or wider life. Gently guide the conversation towards the idea that certificates, scores or final achievements often take centre-stage, while the effort behind them can be overlooked. Introduce the message that qualities such as patience, persistence and problem solving are strong indicators of growth and emotional resilience. Ask each to think of something they have been working on: this might be an academic task, a personal skill or an emotional goal.

Provide a steps-to-success sheet with three sections, 'My goal or challenge', 'The steps I took' and 'What I'm proud of'. Offer quiet reflection time and encourage them to write or draw. Emphasise attention to strategies, small decisions and moments of perseverance rather than outcomes. When ready, invite them to share one process they are proud of. Model process-focused praise, for example, "You tried different approaches until you found what helped", or "You showed real determination when things were tough." Reinforce that every step counts.

Discussion Prompts

Use these prompts to encourage reflection on how valuing effort and gradual improvement can strengthen resilience and support a healthier approach to challenge.

- How did it feel to focus on effort rather than the final result?
- What do you notice about the way you improved over time?
- Why is it important to celebrate the process of learning?
- How might this mindset support you when challenges arise?

Extension or Adaptation Options

Younger children may benefit from using stickers, emoji faces or simple symbols to mark moments of effort on an 'Effort Wall', helping them recognise persistence in a way that feels accessible and motivating. Sentence starters such as "I tried hard when . . ." or "I felt proud when . . ." can further scaffold their reflection. Older children could deepen the activity by writing a short reflective paragraph or composing a note to their future self, outlining how they plan to apply the strategies used on their mountain to future challenges.

Connecting the Learning

Goal setting is a central mechanism through which resilience is developed. When children are supported to identify what matters to them and break this into small, achievable steps, they begin to experience progress as something within their influence. This sense of agency is critical. Repeated experiences of effort leading to change build confidence, support emotional regulation and strengthen persistence over time.

Structured approaches such as the GROW Model provide an effective and developmentally appropriate scaffold. By helping children clarify their goal, reflect on their current reality, explore available options and identify a realistic next step, the model reduces cognitive overload while maintaining purposeful focus. Through this process, self-efficacy is strengthened (Bandura, 1997), motivation is supported through autonomy and competence (Deci and Ryan, 2000), and the importance of clear, appropriately stretching goals is reinforced (Locke and Latham, 2002).

Throughout this unit, the emphasis has been deliberately placed on progress rather than perfection. Children are encouraged to notice effort, recognise incremental improvement and understand that obstacles are a normal and expected part of learning. As they practise reviewing goals, adapting plans and using constructive self-talk, setbacks are reframed as useful information rather than evidence of failure (Dweck, 2006). Research consistently shows that resilience develops through these repeated, supported cycles of challenge, reflection and recovery (Masten, 2014).

This unit also demonstrates how goal setting can actively contribute to inclusion and emotional safety when delivered through a calm, coach-like approach. The activities are designed to support agency without pressure, enabling children to articulate purpose, take ownership of their learning and recognise growth in ways that feel achievable and respectful. When embedded within everyday classroom and pastoral practice, rather than delivered as isolated interventions, these approaches provide predictable structure, support executive functioning and strengthen children's sense of control over their learning and behaviour.

This learning creates a clear bridge into the next unit. While Unit 12 has focused on resilience through purposeful action and self-belief, Unit 13 builds on this foundation by exploring how resilience is further strengthened through connection, meaning and belonging. As children become more confident in directing their own efforts, they are better positioned to recognise their value within relationships and communities. Together, these units reinforce the understanding that resilience is developed not through individual effort alone, but through the interaction of personal agency, supportive relationships and a shared sense of purpose.

Unit 13
Developing Meaning, Purpose and Belonging

- Explore how meaning, purpose and belonging build resilience through challenge and setbacks.
- Develop key skills in self-awareness, motivation and values-led decision making.
- Complete practical reflection and creative tasks such as values-ranking, overlap-circle mapping, role and belonging maps.

Introduction

Resilience develops when children feel genuinely valued, see themselves as capable and know they are connected to the people around them. Fundamental to this process is the development of meaning, purpose and belonging. When children recognise that they have a place within their relationships and communities and when they notice the impact of their own actions, their confidence and emotional security increases. These foundations support them to navigate challenge, recover from setbacks and sustain motivation over time.

In this unit acceptance and achievement are seen not as rewards or grades, but as personal signs of growth that children can recognise in themselves. When they understand that resilience comes from knowing their own worth, noticing their efforts and valuing the steps they take towards goals that matter to them, they begin to feel more confident and secure. By thinking about the people who help them feel seen, supported and safe and by remembering moments that made them proud, they start to join the dots between strong relationships, purposeful action and feeling emotionally steady.

The activities in this unit encourage thoughtful reflection and structured dialogue. Through discussion, guided exercises and creative tasks, children are supported to examine the conditions that help them feel that they matter. As they connect feelings of acceptance with experiences of achievement, they begin to internalise a key message: "I am valued, and what I do has purpose."

DOI: 10.4324/9781003409632-14

Importance of Meaning and Purpose

Children are better able to thrive when they feel their lives have meaning and that their actions make a difference. Developing meaning and purpose is an important part of emotional wellbeing, motivation and resilience. It enables them to look beyond immediate challenges and to recognise that their choices and efforts influence both their own development and the wider world.

Damon, Menon and Bronk (2003, p. 121) define purpose as "a stable and generalised intention to accomplish something that is at once meaningful to the self and of consequence to the world beyond the self". When children understand the why behind what they are doing rather than only the what, they are more likely to maintain motivation, persist with difficulty and experience a stronger sense of connection. Within education settings, meaning and purpose link closely to values-based education.

The Role of Values-Based Education

Values-based Education (VbE), is grounded in the teaching and modelling of universal human values such as kindness, respect, responsibility and empathy. These values contribute to the creation of positive, inclusive cultures in education settings where children experience a sense of belonging, develop secure self-worth and feel motivated to contribute positively to their community.

Values-based Education, pioneered by Dr Neil Hawkes (2005) has become one of the most influential frameworks in this field. Hawkes' model offers a structured ethos, curriculum and set of practices that embed shared values across daily interactions, teaching approaches, leadership decisions and behaviour expectations. Over recent decades, VbE has been adopted by settings both nationally and internationally, with evidence demonstrating its contribution to improved wellbeing, stronger relationships and enhanced learning environments. A values-based approach also provides a practical pathway into exploring meaning and purpose. It encourages children to reflect on fundamental questions such as:

- Who am I?
- What do I stand for?
- How can I make a difference?
- What kind of person do I want to be?

Research by Lovat et al. (2009) highlights that education settings implementing values-based practices often report improvements in behaviour, relationships and emotional wellbeing. When children have opportunities to discuss and apply their values, they begin to internalise them, turning abstract concepts such as respect or responsibility into everyday choices. VbE also strengthens reflection through structured discussion, journalling and collaborative projects. Children make sense of their experiences and understand how their personal goals connect with wider community or global aims.

Building Resilience Through Meaning and Purpose

Resilience develops not only through coping with adversity but also through having something positive to work towards. When children identify what gives their lives meaning they are more willing to show persistence, optimism and confidence when facing challenges (Masten, 2014). Having a purpose also provides them with direction and helps maintain motivation even when circumstances feel uncertain.

Bandura's (1997) theory of self-efficacy highlights the importance of believing that one's actions have impact. When children feel capable of influencing outcomes, they are more resilient during setbacks. Dweck's (2006) work on growth mindset helps them understand this, that mistakes and setbacks are part of learning rather than signs of failure. Meaning and purpose also relate to emotional intelligence (Goleman, 1995): when children reflect on their values, goals and contributions they develop greater self-awareness and empathy. These skills support emotional regulation and promote a stronger sense of identity, helping them respond thoughtfully rather than react impulsively under pressure.

Creating Opportunities for Purpose

Developing meaning and purpose is most effective when opportunities are deliberately planned. Education settings can support this by creating experiences in which children can see the impact of their actions, contribute to something wider than themselves and understand what matters to them: this can be achieved by implementing the following approaches:

- Offering responsibility such as class ambassadors, peer mentors or 'Resilience Warriors' to help promote accountability, pride and belonging.
- Encouraging service and volunteering; for example community contributions strengthen empathy and demonstrate how an individual's effort benefits others.
- Exploring personal values such as circle time, reflection activities or guided conversations helps them understand what is important to them.
- Setting meaningful goals by linking them to personal values helps maintain motivation, for example, "I want to improve my reading so I can help my younger brother."
- Celebrating contribution can be achieved by sharing examples of compassion, leadership or perseverance, building a culture where meaning and purpose are acknowledged.

Practical Ways to Teach Meaning and Purpose

The following activities last between 20 and 40 minutes and are designed for children aged 7 to 14, with adaptations made as needed for younger or older children. Each activity is structured under the following headings, Purpose, Instructions, Discussion Prompts, and Extension or Adaptation. It is important to maintain emotional safety by ensuring that all contributions are respected and valued and by reinforcing that resilience grows through experience and reflection rather than through perfection.

Activity: Things That Matter to Me

Purpose

This activity supports children to identify the personal values that guide their behaviour, influence their choices and underpin their resilience. When they recognise what matters most to them, they develop stronger self-awareness, a clearer sense of purpose and a steadier foundation for navigating challenge and change.

Instructions

Create a calm, reflective atmosphere where children feel safe and able to think openly. Introduce the idea that values guide how we act, respond and make decisions. Explain that knowing our values can act like an internal compass, helping us stay steady when things feel uncertain. Begin with a brief discussion by asking, "What are the things that matter most to you, the things that make you feel proud, connected or true to yourself?" Allow time for sharing and gently draw attention to any common themes that emerge.

Provide each child with a set of value words, for example honesty, kindness, courage, fairness, creativity, friendship, independence and learning. Ask them first to choose ten values that feel meaningful to them, then to narrow these down to five core values. Invite them to rank these five from 1 (most important) to 5. Support children who find ranking difficult by encouraging them to think about which values influence their actions most often.

Next, invite them to place or illustrate their five values inside a simple outline such as a heart, shield or tree. This visual representation helps anchor their choices in a sense of identity and personal strength. Finish by inviting them to share one or two of their values and explain why they matter, reinforcing that every set of values is unique and equally valid.

Discussion Prompts

Use these questions to help them think about the values that matter to them and how those values can guide their choices, feelings and actions.

- Which values were the easiest for you to pick and which ones were a bit harder?
- How do you show your values in your everyday life?
- How could your values help you stay calm or steady when things feel tough?
- Can you think of a recent time when you showed one of your values?
- How do you think it would feel if you did something that went against one of your values?

Extension or Adaptation Options

For younger children use picture-based value cards, short role-play scenarios or simple stories to help them understand values in real, concrete ways. This makes the idea of values more relatable and easier to grasp. For older children introduce a simple weekly 'values in action' journal. This gives them space to think about when they used their values, what felt challenging and what they want to focus on next week. In one-to-one work, link values directly to their current challenges such as friendship worries, tricky decisions or moments when they feel upset or unsure. This helps them see how their values can guide them in real situations. To encourage home-setting communication, invite them to share their top three values with family members.

Activity: Valued and Accepted

Purpose

This activity helps children identify how acceptance from others and meaningful achievements contribute to resilience. It helps them reflect on their sense of belonging, pride and self-worth, all of which play an important role in building emotional strength.

Instructions

Create a calm working environment and explain that acceptance involves feeling seen, respected and welcomed, while achievement involves completing something purposeful that brings satisfaction. Offer examples such as trusted friendships, encouraging adults or helping others. Begin with two questions: "Can you think of a time when someone's encouragement mattered to you?" and "Why did that person's opinion matter?"

Draw attention to key themes such as being valued, supported and feeling capable. Reinforce that resilience develops through connection with others as well as through personal effort. Introduce the two circles of value. Provide paper and ask them to draw two overlapping circles, one labelled 'People whose approval matters to me' and the other 'Tasks or achievements that matter to me'. Title the two circles which overlap with 'Where I feel valued and accepted', then guide them through three steps:

Step 1: Identify people whose acceptance matters and describe what makes their support meaningful.
Step 2: List activities or achievements linked to pride, for example, helping at home, completing a project, showing kindness.
Step 3: Identify moments that sit in the overlap, such as a trusted adult noticing genuine effort or a friend appreciating honesty.

Encourage reflection on why these experiences strengthen confidence and connection. Help them notice how it feels when someone recognises their effort, listens to them or includes them and draw out the link between those moments and feeling more willing to try, learn or take part. Highlight that when children understand why certain people or experiences help them feel valued, they begin to see that resilience grows through both relationships and the choices they make.

Discussion Prompts

Use these prompts to guide them in reflecting on acceptance, recognition and the moments that shape their sense of self-worth.

- How do you know when someone accepts you?
- Which achievements make you feel proud and why?
- How does it feel when someone notices your effort?
- Can you think of a time when recognition was missing? What helped you keep going?

Extension or Adaptation Options

Younger children may express their ideas through drawings, symbols or photos rather than written lists, allowing them to explore feelings of acceptance and achievement in a more concrete and accessible way. Older children can take the activity further by setting a small, realistic personal goal linked to the achievements they identified, helping them connect recognition with motivation and forward action. Families can adapt the activity at home by sharing what they value in one another and noticing moments when encouragement, effort or kindness has made a positive difference, strengthening the link between belonging, recognition and resilience.

Activity: Meaningful Roles

Purpose

This activity helps children recognise the roles they have in different contexts and the places and relationships where they feel they belong. Making these connections visible supports confidence, emotional resilience and self-worth.

Instructions

Begin with a short discussion about the many roles they take on, for example, being a friend, family member, helper or team member. Explore what belonging feels like using terms such as accepted, valued and included. Highlight that roles and belonging strengthen resilience by promoting connection and purpose. Provide each with an A4 sheet titled 'My Roles and Belonging Map'. Ask them to draw a central circle labelled 'Me', surrounded by three circles labelled 'People who are important to me', 'Groups or communities I am part of', 'Places where I feel comfortable'.

In each circle ask them to respond to these three prompts while thinking about at home, in their setting and in their community. Encourage the use of colour coding, symbols, or drawings to personalise their circle map. Allow quiet time for reflection before offering an opportunity for those who wish to share their map with the group.

Discussion Prompts

Use these discussion prompts to help them explore the roles they hold and reflect on how these roles shape their sense of meaning, belonging and resilience.

- Which of your roles feels most important to you and why?
- Which of your roles helps you most when things feel hard and why?
- Which role make you feel happy or gives you energy?
- Who depends on you and how do you help them?
- Where do you feel most welcome and included?
- Who helps you feel like you matter and how do you help others feel they belong?

Extension or Adaptation Options

Younger children may prefer to show their ideas through simple symbols, drawings or pictures rather than written words. Older children can take the activity further by choosing one role they would like to strengthen or develop and thinking about small steps they could take. In group settings they might create a shared 'Belonging Wall' where everyone adds examples of roles, communities or places that help them feel included. In SEND/ALN or alternative provision, use clear visuals, supported reflection and structured prompts to help them express their ideas in a way that feels accessible and comfortable.

Activity: The Resilience Badge

Purpose

This activity supports children in identifying their strengths, values and everyday strategies for staying steady under pressure. Designing a personal 'Resilience Badge' offers a visual reminder that they can adapt, persevere and encourage others.

Instructions

Introduce the 'Resilience Badge' as a personal emblem showing what helps them stay strong and how they support others. Provide a badge template or A4 paper divided into two sections. On the left, ask them to write five practical tips they would give someone struggling for example statements such as keep trying, talk to someone you trust, notice small wins. On the right design their badge using colours, shapes and words linked to their strengths or experiences. Explain that symbols can help us show who we are, what we value and where we feel we belong. Encourage them to include a motto or a meaningful image but reassure them that there is no right way for their badge to look. When they have finished, support them in deciding how they would like to use or display their badge, for example, as a wearable pin, a laminated card or part of a wellbeing display.

Discussion Prompts

Use the following discussion prompts to help them reflect on their resilience badge and explore how these ideas apply in their everyday lives.

- What do the colours, words or symbols on your badge represent?
- Which of your five tips feels most useful at the moment?
- How might your badge encourage someone else?
- In what ways do you see yourself as resilient?
- How could these ideas support you at your setting, home or with friends?

Extension or Adaptation Options

Younger children may enjoy using pre-cut shapes, stickers or collage materials to create their badge, allowing them to express their ideas in a hands-on and creative way. Older children can take the activity further by working collaboratively to create a group resilience charter or by supporting younger children with their badge designs, helping to reinforce shared values and peer encouragement. In one-to-one sessions, link the symbols, words or messages on the badge to specific coping strategies the child already uses or is learning, helping them make clear connections between their strengths and everyday challenges. Families might create a shared badge at home to highlight their collective strengths and the ways they support one another, strengthening a sense of belonging and mutual resilience.

Activity: Becoming A Resilience Warrior

Purpose

This activity helps children consider what it means to be a 'Resilience Warrior', which is someone who shows empathy, courage, patience and steady leadership when situations feel challenging. This helps them recognise how their actions can strengthen resilience in their peer group and wider community.

Instructions

Introduce the idea that a 'Resilience Warrior' is not defined by being the strongest or the loudest but by showing calm, kind and thoughtful support when others find things difficult. Explain that resilience grows when it is shared and that encouragement benefits both the giver and the receiver. Begin with a values-focused discussion using prompts such as, "What does a Resilience Warrior stand for?" or "How might they behave when things feel challenging?" Record key discussion points, drawing attention to empathy, perseverance, fairness and practical problem solving.

Provide two or three short, realistic scenarios, for example, "I can't do this," feeling left out or a friend becoming overwhelmed. Ask, "How might a Resilience Warrior respond?" Encourage simple, achievable actions that demonstrate steady leadership.

Next, explore how resilience messages could be shared across the setting or community. Discuss how gratitude, encouragement and inclusion build confidence. Ask them, "How can you help others feel stronger?" and "What good change would you like to help make happen?" Support them to choose next steps such as creating posters, planning a kindness action, mentoring younger children or preparing a short digital message. Finish by co-producing a 'Resilience Warrior Charter' with three to five core values or actions.

Discussion Prompts

Use the following discussion prompts to explore how confidence, kindness and resilience shape the way we support ourselves and others.

- What helps you feel brave enough to help someone else?
- How does being kind change the way a group acts together?
- What might make it hard for someone to keep going when things are tough and how could we help them?
- How does saying or hearing encouraging things help you stay strong when things are difficult?

Extension or Adaptation Options

Younger children may enjoy expressing their ideas through artwork, simple poems or creating 'Resilience Shields'. Older children could take the activity further by taking on peer support roles, designing wellbeing campaigns or producing digital resources to encourage others. In one-to-one sessions they can create personal resilience pledges and revisit these over time. Families can share real-life examples of resilience to strengthen the home setting link. Whole-setting approaches might include developing 'Resilience Ambassadors' who help promote positive messages across the community.

Activity: Finding Purpose in Everyday Challenges

Purpose

This activity helps education settings create a shared culture where meaning, purpose and contribution shape everyday practice. When children understand how their actions connect to who they hope to become, they are more likely to stay motivated, manage challenges and develop resilient habits.

Instructions

Begin by introducing meaning and purpose as protective factors that support motivation and direction. Engage with a discussion using two guiding questions: "Where in our day do you already do things that feel important or helpful?" and "What could you do to make your day feel even more meaningful or exciting?" Structure the discussion around four themes:

- Reflection: end-of-day or end-of-week check-ins, gratitude practices or conversations with a mentor.
- Connecting learning to life: linking curriculum content to real world issues, possible careers or community needs.
- Empowering voice: creating opportunities for them to contribute to decisions or lead initiatives.
- Modelling purpose: demonstrating through adult behaviour the values and expectations that underpin the setting.

Invite the group to capture their ideas on flipcharts or in a shared digital space. Support them to review the suggestions together and agree on two or three practical actions to trial over the next month. Examples might include creating a 'purpose in action' display that highlights meaningful moments from the week or adding short reflective questions into daily routines or transitions. After the four-week trial, revisit the agreed actions with the group and reflect on their impact on motivation, engagement and sense of purpose.

Discussion Prompts

Use the following prompts to deepen reflection on what matters to them, how connected they feel and what helps the environment thrive.

- What's really important to you when you're at your setting or at home each day?
- When do you feel proud of something you've done?
- How do grown-ups show the values we've been talking about and when do they not show them?
- What helps you feel interested in your learning and part of what's going on?
- What do we already do well here and what do you think we could make even better?

Extension or Adaptation Options

Younger children can explore meaning and purpose through simple stories, play-based activities, or drawings that help them identify what feels important to them. Older children may extend this by linking their learning to future pathways, interests or leadership opportunities within the setting. In one-to-one sessions they can map out their own purpose journey to identify personal goals and motivations. Families can also be involved by sharing examples of purpose and meaningful activities from everyday life.

Connecting the Learning

Developing meaning, purpose and belonging helps children move beyond simply knowing what to do, towards understanding why their actions matter. When children experience opportunities to contribute, reflect and connect with shared values, they begin to see themselves as active participants in their own lives and communities. This sense of agency strengthens the protective factors that underpin resilience, including self-efficacy (Bandura, 1997), a growth mindset (Dweck, 2006) and emotional intelligence (Goleman, 1995).

Meaning and purpose provide direction and motivation, particularly during moments of uncertainty or challenge. Belonging provides the relational safety that enables children to persevere, take risks and recover from setbacks. Together, these elements help children develop a secure sense of self, rooted in the understanding that they are valued and capable, and that their actions have impact.

Approaches such as Values-based Education, meaningful roles, service opportunities and the recognition of contribution reinforce a consistent message: "You matter, and what you do makes a difference." When this message is experienced through everyday interactions rather than delivered as a slogan, children are more likely to internalise it. Feeling seen, listened to and respected supports emotional wellbeing and identity development, helping children to navigate relationships and challenges with greater confidence.

Adults play a critical role in making these connections visible. By modelling shared values, noticing effort rather than perfection and creating inclusive environments, they help children link their daily choices to the people they are becoming. In doing so, resilience is not taught as a skill to be mastered, but nurtured as a lived experience grounded in connection, purpose and belonging.

RESOURCES

Assessments

The following validated assessment tools are widely used in educational and psychosocial settings to support the identification, monitoring and evaluation of children's emotional well-being, behaviour, and resilience.

Strengths and Difficulties Questionnaire (SDQ). Goodman, R. Available at: https://www.sdqinfo.org/

The Child and Youth Resilience Measure (CYRM). Resilience Research Centre. Available at: https://resilienceresearch.org/home-cyrm/

The Warwick-Edinburgh Mental Wellbeing Scale (WEMWBS). Tennant, R. et al. (2007) Available at: https://www.corc.uk.net/media/1537/wemwbs.pdf

Frameworks & Schemes

The following frameworks and schemes provide structured, practice informed approaches for developing emotional literacy, resilience and self-regulation in children across educational settings.

Family Growth Mindset Scheme. NSM Training & Consultancy. Available at: https://nsmtc.co.uk/resource/family-growth-mindset-scheme-pack/

Family Values Scheme. NSM Training & Consultancy. Available at: https://nsmtc.co.uk/resource/the-family-values-scheme/

Resilience Framework for Children and Young People. Boingboing Resilience CIC. Available at: https://www.boingboing.org.uk/boingboing-resilience-framework-children-young-people/

The Zones of Regulation. Kuypers, L.M. Available at: https://zonesofregulation.com

Values-based Education (VbE). Available at: https://www.valuesbasededucation.com

Academic Books and Resources

The following academic texts contribute to current understanding of resilience, motivation, wellbeing and learning and provide evidence-informed perspectives to support effective practice with children in educational settings.

Character, grit and resilience pocketbook. Simister, C.J. (2017). Teachers' Pocketbooks.

Flourish: A visionary new understanding of happiness and well-being. Seligman, M.E.P. (2011). Free Press.

Grit: The power of passion and perseverance. Duckworth, A. (2016). Vermilion.

How will I ever get through this? A practical guide to navigating life's toughest times. Hone, L. (2026). Allen & Unwin.

Learned optimism: How to change your mind and your life. Seligman, M.E.P. (2006). Vintage Books.

Mindset: The new psychology of success. Dweck, C.S. (2006). Random House.

Mindset: Changing the way you think to fulfil your potential. Dweck, C.S. (2017). Robinson.

Raising an emotionally intelligent child. Gottman, J. & DeClaire, J. (1997). Simon & Schuster.

Resilient grieving: Finding strength and embracing life after a loss that changes everything. Hone, L. (2018). The Experiment.

The learning challenge: How to guide students through the learning pit. Nottingham, J. (2017). Corwin.

The learning power approach: Teaching learners to teach themselves. Claxton, G. (2018). Crown House Publishing.

The Developing Mind. Siegel D. J. (2012). Guilford Press.

The educators' guide to whole-school wellbeing: A practical guide to getting started, best-practice process and effective implementation. Quinlan, D.M. and Hone, L.C. (2020). Routledge.

The whole-brain child: 12 revolutionary strategies to nurture your child's developing mind. Siegel, D.J. and Bryson, T.P. (2011). Delacorte Press.

What works in promoting social and emotional wellbeing and responding to mental health problems in schools. Weare, K. (2015). National Children's Bureau.

TED Talks

The following TED and TEDx talks offer accessible, real-world insights into resilience, perseverance, mindset and motivation and can be used to stimulate reflection and discussion in professional learning and educational settings.

The Three Secrets of Resilient People. Lucy Hone. (2019), TEDx. Available at https://www.youtube.com/watch?v=NWH8N-BvhAw

Unfinished Business: Delaying the Urge to Give Up. Morgan, N.S. (2023). TEDx. Available at: https://www.youtube.com/watch?v=H3clvW2GIXY

Never, Ever Give Up. Nyad, D. (2013). TED. Available at: https://www.ted.com/talks/diana_nyad_never_ever_give_up

Story Books

The following age-appropriate story books use narrative to explore themes of resilience, identity, belonging, perseverance and emotional growth. These can be used to support discussion, reflection and emotional literacy with children.

Ages 3 to 7

Some dogs do. Alborough, J. (2011). Walker Books.
Giraffes can't dance. Andreae, G. (1999). Orchard Books.
Cleversticks. Ashley, B. (2001). Crown/Orchard Books.
Your fantastic elastic brain. Deak, J. (2010). Little Pickle Press.
Dogs don't do ballet. Kemp, A. (2004). Simon & Schuster Children's Books.
The girl who never made mistakes. Pett, M., & Rubinstein, G. (2010). Sourcebooks Jabberwocky.
The dot. Reynolds, P. H. (2003). Candlewick Press.
Ish. Reynolds, P. H. (2004). Candlewick Press.
The most magnificent thing. Spires, A. (2014). Kids Can Press.
What do you do with an idea? Yamada, K. (2014). Compendium.
What do you do with a problem? Yamada, K. (2016). Compendium.

Ages 8 to 12

El Deafo. Bell, C. (2014). Amulet Books.
Across the desert. Bowling, D. (2018). Little, Brown Books for Young Readers.
New kid. Craft, J. (2019). Quill Tree Books.
Out of my mind. Draper, S. M. (2010). Atheneum Books for Young Readers.
The remarkable journey of Coyote Sunrise. Gemeinhart, D. (2019). Henry Holt and Company.
Real friends. Hale, S. (2017). First Second Books.
Fish in a tree. Hunt, L. M. (2015). Nancy Paulsen Books.
When stars are scattered. Jamieson, V., & Mohamed, O. (2018). Dial Books for Young Readers.
The boy who harnessed the wind. Kamkwamba, W., & Mealer, B. (2015). Puffin Books.
Mirette on the high wire. McCully, E. A. (1992). G. P. Putnam's Sons.
Pax. Pennypacker, S. (2016). Balzer + Bray.
The red pencil. Pinkney, A. T. (2014). Little, Brown Books for Young Readers.
Amal unbound. Saeed, A. (2018). Nancy Paulsen Books.
Counting by 7s. Sloan, H. (2013). Dial Books for Young Readers.

Ages 13 to 18

Shout. Anderson, L. H. (2019). Viking Books for Young Readers.
The stress survival guide for teens. Bernstein, J. (2016). Free Spirit Publishing.
Apple: Skin to the core. Gansworth, E. (2020). Milkweed Editions.
Call me American. Iftin, A. N. (2018). Alfred A. Knopf.
13 things strong kids do. Morin, A. (2017). HarperCollins.
Ain't burned all the bright. Reynolds, J., & Griffin, S. (2022). Atheneum Books for Young Readers.
We are not from here. Sanchez Torres, J. (2020). Philomel Books.
Scars like wings. Stewart, E. (2020). Delacorte Press.
Somebody give this heart a pen. Thakur, S. (2021). Penguin Workshop.
Before the ever after. Woodson, J. (2020). Nancy Paulsen Books.

Films

The following films depict real and fictional narratives of perseverance, identity and resilience. These can be used as reflective resources to support discussion about challenge, failure and personal growth in educational and professional learning contexts.

Akeelah and the Bee. Atchison, D. (2006). USA: Lionsgate.
Eddie the Eagle. Fletcher, D. (2016). UK: Marv Films.
Freedom Writers. LaGravenese, R. (2007). USA: Paramount Pictures.
The Great Debaters. Washington, D. (2007). USA: Harpo Productions.
Inside Out. Docter, P. (Dir.) (2015) Film. United States: Pixar Animation Studios.
Kung Fu Panda. Stevenson, J. and Osborne, M. (Dirs.) (2008) Film. United States: DreamWorks Animation.
The Other Shore: The Diana Nyad Story. Wheeler, T. (2013). USA: HBO Sports.
The Young Woman and the Sea. Rønning, J. (2024). USA: Walt Disney Studios Motion Pictures.

YouTube Clips

The following short video clips provide accessible visual prompts to reinforce messages about perseverance, growth mindset and resilience. These can be used to support discussion and reflection with children in educational settings.

Don't Give Up. Mars, B. Sesame Street. Available at: https://www.youtube.com/watch?v=pWp6kkz-pnQ
Power of Yet. Monáe, J. Sesame Street. Available at: https://www.youtube.com/watch?v=XLeUvZvuvAs
Famous Failures: Never Give Up. Available at: https://www.youtube.com/watch?v=5cZh6tYVM2w
Derek Redmond's 1992 Olympic 400m Race. Available at: https://www.youtube.com/watch?v=yrboO72eJKg

Keynotes & Training

Nicola S. Morgan delivers keynotes and professional training on resilience for education and organisational settings. Sessions are available face to face or live online.

For further information, contact hello@nicolasmorgan.com or visit www.nicolasmorgan.com.

For CPD Certified resilience training, visit www.nsmtc.co.uk.

REFERENCES

Allen, K.A., Kern, M.L., Vella-Brodrick, D. and Waters, L. (2018). What schools need to know about fostering school belonging: A meta-analysis. *Educational Psychology Review*, 30(1), pp. 1–34.

American Psychological Association (2014). *The road to resilience*. Washington, DC: American Psychological Association.

American Psychological Association (2020). *Building your resilience*. Washington, DC: American Psychological Association.

Andreas, S. and Faulkner, C. (1994). *NLP: the new technology of achievement*. New York: William Morrow.

Bandler, R. and Grinder, J. (1979). *Frogs into princes: neuro-linguistic programming*. Moab, UT: Real People Press.

Bandura, A. (1986). *Social foundations of thought and action: A social cognitive theory*. Englewood Cliffs, NJ: Prentice Hall.

Bandura, A. (1997). *Self-efficacy: The exercise of control*. New York: W.H. Freeman.

Baumeister, R.F. and Leary, M.R. (1995). The need to belong: Desire for interpersonal attachments as a fundamental human motivation. *Psychological Bulletin*, 117(3), pp. 497–529.

Baumrind, D. (1991). The influence of parenting style on adolescent competence and substance use. *Journal of Early Adolescence*, 11(1), pp. 56–95.

Bellis, M.A., Hughes, K., Leckenby, N., Perkins, C. and Lowey, H. (2014). *National household survey of adverse childhood experiences and their relationship with resilience to health-harming behaviours*. Cardiff: Public Health Wales.

Benard, B. (2004). *Resiliency: What we have learned*. San Francisco: WestEd.

Blakemore, S.J. (2018). *Inventing ourselves: The secret life of the teenage brain*. London: Doubleday.

Boingboing (n.d.). *Resilience Framework for Children and Young People*. Available at: https://www.boingboing.org.uk (Accessed: 15 April 2026).

Bowlby, J. (1988). *A secure base: Parent-child attachment and healthy human development*. London: Routledge.

Bransford, J.D., Brown, A.L. and Cocking, R.R. (2000). *How people learn: Brain, mind, experience, and school*. Washington, DC: National Academy Press.

Bronfenbrenner, U. (1979). *The ecology of human development: experiments by nature and design*. Cambridge, MA: Harvard University Press.

Bronfenbrenner, U. (2005). *Making human beings human: Bioecological perspectives on human development*. Thousand Oaks, CA: Sage.

Brooks, R. (2006). *The power of parenting*. Boston, MA: Da Capo Press.

Coburn, A. and Gormally, S. (2017). *Wellbeing in schools: A whole school approach*. London: Jessica Kingsley Publishers.

Collaborative for Academic, Social, and Emotional Learning (2020). *What is social and emotional learning?* Chicago, IL: CASEL.

Compas, B.E., Jaser, S.S., Bettis, A.H., Watson, K.H., Gruhn, M.A., Dunbar, J.P., Williams, E.K. and Thigpen, J.C. (2017). *Coping, emotion regulation, and psychopathology in childhood and adolescence*. Washington, DC: American Psychological Association.

Damon, W. (2008). *The path to purpose*. New York: Free Press.

Damon, W., Menon, J. and Bronk, K.C. (2003). The development of purpose during adolescence. *Applied Developmental Science*, 7(3), pp. 119–128.

Daniel, B. and Wassell, S. (2002). Adolescence: *Assessing and promoting resilience in vulnerable children*. London: Jessica Kingsley Publishers.

Darling-Hammond, L., Flook, L., Cook-Harvey, C., Barron, B. and Osher, D. (2019). *Implications for educational practice of the science of learning and development*. Palo Alto, CA: Learning Policy Institute.

Deci, E.L. and Ryan, R.M. (2000). Intrinsic and extrinsic motivations: Classic definitions and new directions. *Contemporary Educational Psychology*, 25(1), pp. 54–67.

Denham, S.A. (2006). Social-emotional competence as support for school readiness, in McCartney, K. and Phillips, D. (eds.) *Blackwell handbook of early childhood development*. Oxford: Blackwell, pp. 85–103.

Denham, S.A., Bassett, H.H. and Wyatt, T. (2012). *The socialization of emotional competence*. New York: Guilford Press.

Department for Education (2018). *Mental health and behaviour in schools*. London: Department for Education.

Diamond, A. (2013). Executive functions. *Annual Review of Psychology*, 64, pp. 135-168.

Durlak, J.A., Weissberg, R.P., Dymnicki, A.B., Taylor, R.D. and Schellinger, K.B. (2011). The impact of enhancing students' social and emotional learning. *Child Development*, 82(1), pp. 405–432.

Dweck, C.S. (2006). *Mindset: The new psychology of success*. New York: Random House.

Dweck, C.S. (2017). *Mindset: Changing the way you think to fulfil your potential*. London: Robinson.

D'Zurilla, T. J. and Nezu, A. M. (2010). Problem-solving therapy, in Dobson, K.S. (ed.), *Handbook of cognitive-behavioral therapies*. New York: Guilford Press, pp. 197–225.

Eccles, J.S. and Gootman, J.A. (2002). *Community programs to promote youth development*. Washington, DC: National Academy Press.

Eccles, J.S. and Roeser, R.W. (2011). Schools as developmental contexts during adolescence, *Journal of Research on Adolescence*, 21(1), pp. 225–241.

Emmons, R.A. and McCullough, M.E. (2003). Counting blessings versus burdens: An experimental investigation of gratitude and subjective well-being in daily life. *Journal of Personality and Social Psychology*, 84(2), pp. 377-389.

Epstein, J.L. (2011). *School, family, and community partnerships*. 2nd ed. Boulder, CO: Westview Press.

Evans, G.W. and Kim, P. (2013). Childhood poverty, chronic stress, self-regulation, and coping, *Child Development Perspectives*, 7(1), pp. 43–48.

Felitti, V.J., Anda, R.F., Nordenberg, D., Williamson, D.F., Spitz, A.M., Edwards, V., Koss, M.P. and Marks, J.S. (1998). Relationship of childhood abuse and household dysfunction to leading causes of death. *American Journal of Preventive Medicine*, 14(4), pp. 245–258.

Flavell, J.H. (1979). Metacognition and cognitive monitoring: A new area of cognitive-developmental inquiry, *American Psychologist*, 34(10), pp. 906–911.

Fredrickson, B.L. (2001). The broaden-and-build theory of positive emotions. *American Psychologist*, 56(3), pp. 218-226.

Gathercole, S.E. and Alloway, T.P. (2008). *Working memory and learning: A practical guide for teachers*. London: Sage Publications.

Gilligan, R. (2009). *Promoting resilience: Supporting children and young people who are in care, adopted or in need*. London: British Association for Adoption and Fostering.

Goleman, D. (1995). *Emotional intelligence*. New York: Bantam Books.

Goodall, J. and Montgomery, C. (2014). Parental involvement to parental engagement: A continuum, *Educational Review*, 66(4), pp. 399–410.

Grotberg, E.H. (1997). *The International Resilience Project: Findings from the research and the effectiveness of interventions*. Washington, DC: Civitan International Research Center, University of Alabama at Birmingham.

Gross, J.J. (2015). *Handbook of emotion regulation*. 2nd ed. New York: Guilford Press.

Hamre, B.K. and Pianta, R.C. (2006). Student-teacher relationships, in Alexander, P.A. and Winne, P.H. (eds.) *Handbook of educational psychology* (2nd edn). Mahwah, NJ: Lawrence Erlbaum Associates, pp. 685-703.

Hart, S. and Blincow, D. (2007). *Resilient therapy*. London: Routledge.

Hartley, M.T. (2011). Examining the relationships between resilience, mental health, and academic persistence in undergraduate college students. *Journal of American College Health*, 59(7), pp. 596–604.

Hattie, J. and Yates, G. (2014). *Visible learning and the science of how we learn*. London: Routledge.

Hawkes, N. (2005). Does teaching values improve the quality of education in primary schools? Unpublished doctoral thesis. Oxford University, Oxford.

Immordino-Yang, M.H. and Damasio, A. (2007). We feel, therefore we learn. *Mind, Brain, and Education*, 1(1), pp. 3–10.

Jennings, P.A. and Greenberg, M.T. (2009). The prosocial classroom: Teacher social and emotional competence in relation to student and classroom outcomes, *Review of Educational Research*, 79(1), pp. 491–525.

Keyes, C.L.M. (2019). The mental health continuum: From languishing to flourishing in life. *Journal of Health and Social Behavior*, 60(3), pp. 321–337.

Kuypers, L.M. (2011). *The zones of regulation: A curriculum designed to foster self-regulation and emotional control*. San Jose, CA: Think Social Publishing.

Kuypers, L.M. (2024). *Getting into the zones of regulation: The complete framework and digital curriculum companion*. San Jose, CA: Think Social Publishing.

Ladson-Billings, G. (1995). Toward a theory of culturally relevant pedagogy, *American Educational Research Journal*, 32(3), pp. 465–491.

Lazarus, R.S. and Folkman, S. (1984). *Stress, appraisal, and coping*. New York: Springer.

Leithwood, K., Harris, A. and Hopkins, D. (2020). Seven strong claims about successful school leadership revisited, *School Leadership & Management*, 40(1), pp. 5–22.

Lerner, R.M., Almerigi, J.B., Theokas, C. and Lerner, J.V. (2005). Positive youth development: A view of the issues, *Journal of Early Adolescence*, 25(1), pp. 10–16.

Loades, M.E., Chatburn, E., Higson-Sweeney, N., Reynolds, S., Shafran, R., Brigden, A., Linney, C., McManus, M.N., Borwick, C. and Crawley, E. (2020). Rapid systematic review: The impact of social isolation and loneliness on the mental health of children and adolescents in the context of COVID-19, *Journal of the American Academy of Child & Adolescent Psychiatry*, 59(11), pp. 1218–1239.e3.

Locke, E.A. and Latham, G.P. (2002). Building a practically useful theory of goal setting and task motivation: A 35-year odyssey. *American Psychologist*, 57(9), pp. 705–717.

Lovat, T., Toomey, R., Clement, N., Crotty, R., Nielsen, T. and Dally, K. (2009). *Values education, quality teaching and service learning: A troika for effective teaching and learning*. Terrigal, NSW: David Barlow Publishing.

Luthar, S.S., Cicchetti, D. and Becker, B. (2000). The construct of resilience. *Child Development*, 71(3), pp. 543–562.

Luthar, S.S., Crossman, E.J. and Small, P.J. (2015). Resilience and adversity, in Lamb, M.E. (ed.) *Handbook of child psychology and developmental science* (7th edn). Hoboken, NJ: John Wiley & Sons, pp. 247–286.

Mapp, K.L. and Kuttner, P.J. (2013). *Partners in education: A dual capacity-building framework for family-school partnerships*. Austin, TX: Southwest Educational Development Laboratory (SEDL).

Martin, A.J. and Marsh, H.W. (2009). Academic resilience and its psychological and educational correlates: A construct validity approach, *Psychology in the Schools*, 46(3), pp. 267–281.

Masten, A.S. (2014). *Ordinary magic: Resilience in development*. New York: Guilford Press.

Masten, A.S. (2001). Ordinary magic: Resilience processes in development, *American Psychologist*, 56(3), pp. 227–238.

Masten, A.S. and Barnes, A.J. (2018). Resilience in children: Developmental perspectives, *Children*, 5(7), p. 98.

McEwen, B.S. (2017). Neurobiological and systemic effects of chronic stress, *Chronic Stress*, 1, pp. 1–11.

Mehrabian, A. (1972). *Nonverbal communication*. Chicago: Aldine-Atherton.

Mischel, W., Shoda, Y. and Rodriguez, M.L. (1989). Delay of gratification in children. *Science*, 244(4907), pp. 933–938.

Morgan, N.S. (2017). *Engaging Families in Schools: Parents as Co-Educators*. London: Routledge.

Morgan, N.S. (2023). *Unfinished Business: Delaying the Urge to Give Up*. TEDx Talk.

Neff, K.D. (2011). Self-compassion, self-esteem, and well-being, *Social and Personality Psychology Compass*, 5(1), pp. 1–12.

National Scientific Council on the Developing Child (2015). Supportive relationships and active skill-building strengthen the foundations of resilience: Working paper 13. Cambridge, MA: Center on the Developing Child, Harvard University.

New Economics Foundation (2008). *Five ways to wellbeing: The evidence*. London: New Economics Foundation.

NHS Digital (2023). Mental health of children and young people in England, 2023. Leeds: NHS Digital.

NHS Greater Glasgow and Clyde (n.d.). 5-a-day for mental wellbeing. Glasgow: NHS Greater Glasgow and Clyde.

Norrish, J.M., Williams, P., O'Connor, M. and Robinson, J. (2013). An applied framework for positive education. *International Journal of Wellbeing*, 3(2), pp. 147–161.

Ochsner, K.N. and Gross, J.J. (2005). The cognitive control of emotion, *Trends in Cognitive Sciences*, 9(5), pp. 242–249.

Odgers, C.L. and Jensen, M.R. (2020). Annual research review: Adolescent mental health in the digital age: Facts, fears, and future directions, *Journal of Child Psychology and Psychiatry*, 61(3), pp. 336–348.

OECD (2019). *Future of education and skills 2030*. Paris: OECD.

Passmore, J., van Nieuwerburgh, C. and Barr, M. (2019). Workplace coaching, in Griffin, R.W. (ed.) *Oxford bibliographies in management*. New York: Oxford University Press.

Perry, B.D. (2006). Fear and learning: Trauma-related factors in the adult education process, New Directions for *Adult and Continuing Education*, 110, pp. 21–27.

Perry, B.D. and Szalavitz, M. (2017). *The boy who was raised as a dog: And other stories from a child psychiatrist's notebook* (3rd edn). New York: Basic Books.

Pianta, R.C. (1999). *Enhancing relationships between children and teachers*. Washington, DC: American Psychological Association.

Pianta, R.C., Hamre, B.K. and Allen, J.P. (2012). Teacher-student relationships and engagement: Conceptualizing, measuring, and improving the capacity of classroom interactions, in Christenson, S.L., Reschly, A.L. and Wylie, C. (eds.) *Handbook of research on student engagement*. Boston, MA: Springer, pp. 365–386.

Porges, S.W. (2011). *The polyvagal theory*. New York: Norton.

Post, S.G. (2005). Altruism, happiness, and health: It's good to be good, *International Journal of Behavioral Medicine*, 12(2), pp. 66–77.

Public Health England (2019). Promoting children and young people's emotional health and wellbeing: A whole school and college approach. London: Public Health England.

Reivich, K. and Shatté, A. (2002). *The resilience factor: 7 keys to finding your inner strength and overcoming life's hurdles*. New York: Broadway Books.

Riley, P. (2019). The Australian Principal Occupational Health, Safety and Wellbeing Survey 2019 Data. Fitzroy, Victoria: Australian Catholic University.

Rutter, M. (2013). Resilience. *Journal of Child Psychology and Psychiatry*, 54(4), pp. 474–487.

Scales, P.C., Anderson, E.M., Roehlkepartain, E.C., Kielsmeier, J.C. and Benson, P.L. (2018). Effects of developmental relationships with teachers on middle-school students' motivation and performance', *Psychology in the Schools*, 55(6), pp. 646–663.

Scales, P.C., Benson, P.L., Leffert, N. and Blyth, D.A. (2016). Contribution of developmental assets to the prediction of thriving among adolescents, *Applied Developmental Science*, 4(1), pp. 27–46.

Seligman, M.E.P. (2011). *Flourish: A visionary new understanding of happiness and well-being*. New York: Free Press.

Shanker, S. (2016). Self-Reg: *How to help your child (and you) break the stress cycle and successfully engage with life*. Toronto: Penguin Random House Canada.

Sheridan, S.M., Smith, T.E., Kim, E.M., Beretvas, S.N. and Park, S. (2019). A meta-analysis of family-school interventions and children's social-emotional functioning: Moderators and components of efficacy, *Review of Educational Research*, 89(2), pp. 296–332.

Shonkoff, J.P. (2016). Capitalizing on advances in science to reduce the health consequences of early childhood adversity. *JAMA Pediatrics*, 170(10), pp. 1003–1007.

Shonkoff, J.P. (2020). Building a new biodevelopmental framework to guide the future of early childhood policy, *Child Development*, 91(6), pp. 1898–1909.

Shonkoff, J.P., Garner, A.S., Siegel, B.S., Dobbins, M.I., Earls, M.F., McGuinn, L., Pascoe, J. and Wood, D.L. (2012). The lifelong effects of early childhood adversity and toxic stress, *Pediatrics*, 129(1), e232–e246.

Siegel, D.J. (2012). *The developing mind*. 2nd ed. New York: Guilford Press.

Siegel, D.J. and Bryson, T.P. (2011). *The whole-brain child: 12 revolutionary strategies to nurture your child's developing mind*. New York: Random House.

Siegel, D.J. and Bryson, T.P. (2014). *No-drama discipline: The whole-brain way to calm the chaos and nurture your child's developing mind*. New York: Bantam Books.

Skinner, E.A. and Zimmer-Gembeck, M.J. (2016). The development of coping: Stress, neurophysiology, social relationships, and resilience during childhood and adolescence. Cham: Springer.

Snyder, C.R. (2002). Hope theory: Rainbows in the mind. *Psychological Inquiry*, 13(4), pp. 249–275.

Sroufe, L.A. (2005). Attachment and development: A prospective, longitudinal study from birth to adulthood, *Attachment & Human Development*, 7(4), pp. 349–367.

Sugai, G. and Horner, R. (2006). A promising approach for expanding and sustaining school-wide positive behavior support, *School Psychology Review*, 35(2), pp. 245–259.

Twenge, J.M. (2017). *iGen: Why today's super-connected kids are growing up less rebellious, more tolerant, less happy–and completely unprepared for adulthood*. New York: Atria Books.

Ungar, M. (2012). Social ecologies and their contribution to resilience, in Ungar, M. (ed.) *The social ecology of resilience: A handbook of theory and practice*. New York: Springer, pp. 13–31.

Ungar, M. (2015). *Resilience and culture: The diversity of protective processes and positive adaptation*. New York: Springer.

Wang, M.T. and Eccles, J.S. (2012). Social support matters: Longitudinal effects of social support on three dimensions of school engagement from middle to high school. *Child Development*, 83(3), pp. 877–895.

Weare, K. (2015). *What works in promoting social and emotional well-being*. London: National Children's Bureau.

Weare, K. and Nind, M. (2011). Mental health promotion and problem prevention in schools: What does the evidence say?, *Health Promotion International*, 26(S1), pp. i29–i69.

Werner, E.E. and Smith, R.S. (1992). *Overcoming the odds: High risk children from birth to adulthood*. Ithaca, NY: Cornell University Press.

Werner, E.E. and Smith, R.S. (2001). *Journeys from childhood to midlife: Risk, resilience, and recovery*. Ithaca, NY: Cornell University Press.

Whitmore, J. (1992). *Coaching for performance: A practical guide to growing your own skills*. London: Nicholas Brealey Publishing.

World Health Organization (2020). *Guidelines on mental health at work*. Geneva: WHO.

Yeager, D.S. and Dweck, C.S. (2012). Mindsets that promote resilience. *Educational Psychologist*, 47(4), pp. 302–314.

Zelazo, P.D. and Carlson, S.M. (2012). Hot and cool executive function in childhood and adolescence: Development and plasticity, *Child Development Perspectives*, 6(4), pp. 354–360.

Zeldin, S., Christens, B.D. and Powers, J.L. (2013). The psychology and practice of youth-adult partnership: Bridging generations for youth development and community change, *American Journal of Community Psychology*, 51(3–4), pp. 385–397.

Zimmer-Gembeck, M.J. and Skinner, E.A. (2011) Review: The development of coping across childhood and adolescence: An integrative review and critique of research. *International Journal of Behavioral Development*, 35(1), pp. 1–17.

Zimmerman, B.J. (2002). Becoming a self-regulated learner. *Theory Into Practice*, 41(2), pp. 64–70.

INDEX

www.ingramcontent.com/pod-product-compliance
Lightning Source LLC
LaVergne TN
LVHW081115160826
845780LV00029B/246
* 9 7 8 1 0 3 2 5 2 9 9 4 3 *